Stalking: Surviving the Hidden Terror

Stalking:
Surviving the Hidden Terror

D1246244

By Paula LaRue

Stalking: Surviving the Hidden Terror

Library of Congress Cataloging in Publication Data

Published by:

Insight Publishing Company
P.O. Box 4189
Sevierville, TN 37864
Printed in USA

Cover Design By: Douglas Graphics

ISBN No. 1-885640-08-0

Acknowledgments

I would like to acknowledge all the people who contributed to this book including law enforcement professionals, attorneys and psychologists. Without their help, I would never have been able to understand much less communicate, the terrifying nature of stalking.

I would particularly like to thank all the survivors who shared their horrific experiences with me. Their courage and determination to go on with their lives when faced with devastating situations are inspirational to all of us. They truly demonstrate the strength of the human spirit.

In addition, this book is dedicated to my husband, Jack, for all of his love and support throughout this project.

Table Of Contents

STALKING CASE: ONE

**He turned the gun on her and said, "You're going to die bitch."
Then he shot her...**

Carol was 21 when she met John. She lived next door from John's cousin. One day while Carol was digging in her garden, John came over and asked if he could help. She thought he was very charming and that he had the gift of gab. She was attracted to him because he had a "bad boy" look about him. A few days later, he asked her out. Not knowing what the future would bring, she accepted. They dated for a couple of weeks but after a while, they mutually broke up. John was concerned that they were moving too fast and he wanted to go his own way. That was fine for Carol, because she wasn't sure that he was the right one for her anyway. So they stopped dating. (This is an interesting twist in a stalking case. Many times the stalker wants a quick commitment. They try to gain control before the victim knows what is happening.)

A couple of years later, Carol and John met again after he had broken up with his girlfriend. He had been in a bad accident and needed help. John couldn't feed himself, so Carol decided to help him out. This was the beginning of 10 years of living hell...

Carol had a home given to her by a relative. John said he could help her to fix it up. So they decided to live together. About a year later she and John had a son.

During their relationship John wanted her to account for every second of time that she wasn't with him. When she went out, he wanted her to be home at a certain time. If she wasn't home, he would call her mother's house, to see where she was. John wouldn't allow Carol to go to family holiday gatherings. If it was a "pot-luck" dinner, he would knock the dish she was bringing out of her hands so she couldn't take one.

He also followed her to work. He knew exactly when she went to and came back from lunch. If she wasn't home at a certain time he would question her. There were accusations like, "You are cheating on me." or "Who are you seeing at work?" This happened every day.
These were warning signs of stalking, but Carol didn't see his behavior that way. She took it as attention. They'd been in the relationship for awhile and she didn't think what he was doing was wrong. She thought he was paying attention to her. She never had someone care so much about what she did, where she went and who she went with. To Carol, this seemed normal. As the relationship went on, however, the smothering "attention" got overwhelming. She got tired of being asked where she was going and with whom. She didn't like being told who she was allowed to go with. The "attention" got old fast.

Carol had a daughter in 1992. At this time, their relationship was rocky. John became violent. Sometimes he took it out on the car, but other times he took it out on her. Then he started beating the children. One time he hit their son with a two-by-four board across the rear end. Carol had warned John that she didn't want him to hurt the kids, so she eventually kicked him out. Because of the children, John was forced to pay child support. The child support came out of his paycheck. Every time he had to pay, he'd follow her to work.

John then started harassing Carol at work. One day he called her so many times, her boss told her to just go home. One morning Carol was headed to the day care center with one child in the car when John raced his car towards hers. She knew she was in trouble. She thought that he was trying to crash into her. She pulled in front of the day care center. John came towards her car and told her to roll down the window. Carol said she wouldn't because she feared he was going to hit her. He said he wouldn't, that he just wanted to talk. She still said "No". John became infuriated and started banging on the windshield, and busted it. With the day care center close by, Carol started honking the horn to attract attention. That finally caused John to leave.

Carol and John broke up several times. Each time he would always say that he was sorry, and that the violence wouldn't happen again. He would say everything would be "Ok". To make amends he would always offer to pay for any damage that he caused. He did this for the windshield incident. He told her that if she didn't press charges, he'd buy a new windshield. He thought everything would be all right as long as he paid for the damage. John rationalized that if he paid for it, it would erase what he did. If he fixed it, he didn't do it. It was like the violence never happened. That's how the relationship went on for some time.

Another time, Carol and a girlfriend went to a concert. Carol was 8 ½ months pregnant. As they were walking up the steps to the stadium, John suddenly appeared. He grabbed her by the arm and pulled her over to the side. There were police standing nearby, but they didn't notice what was happening. John grabbed Carol's necklace and pulled it off. Then he grabbed her hand, smashing her ring into her hand and said, "You're going home with me". Carol felt bad about leaving, because her girlfriend had paid for the tickets. She said, "No, let me go to the concert. I'll come home after the concert." John said, "No, you're going home with me right now!"

John had ridden his motorcycle to the concert and wanted her to ride on the back of the motorcycle. Carol didn't want to because she was 8-½ mos. pregnant. She wouldn't do it, so her girlfriend ended up leaving with her and driving her home. John was behind them the whole way home - right on the bumper.

Later Carol reflected on what happened. " I will never forget the way people looked at me when he was doing this to me. When I was standing there while he was ripping my necklace off. Here I am 8-½ mos. pregnant and it's a very noticeable scene. I could hear other men cheering him on. I will never forget hearing the voices and the laughter behind him when he did that to me. The police did not move, they were right down the hall and they did not move."

When they got home John started screaming at Carol that she was hurting the baby. He started busting the windows and throwing things around the house. Finally, she kicked him out again. She was tired of the violence. The kids had seen too much of it. She evicted him and filed a restraining order against him. Even though Carol had evicted him, John still wanted to be a part of her life.

Carol kept a log. She documented every time he called and, everytime she saw his van drive by the house. When he followed her she called the police. They seemed interested in helping her, but still did not arrest him.

As time went on Carol met someone else. She hadn't been looking to start a new relationship, but she met someone she liked. She thought that - just maybe - there was hope for a better life for her and her children. John's stalking escalated when he became aware Carol was seeing another man.

One Sunday Carol and her son were going to go shopping. John wanted to go along. He was upset because she was dating someone. John pulled their son aside and said if he saw Carol and her boyfriend together, he'd kill them and kill himself. The son told Carol this the next day as she was getting ready for work.

Suddenly there was pounding on the front door. It was John. Carol didn't want to let him in because of what he had said. She told John to go away or she'd call the police. When he didn't leave, she called the police. But by the time the police arrived, John had gone. He had watched her through the window and when he saw her call, he left. The police asked Carol if she wanted to press charges because he wouldn't leave her alone. She said, "Yes."

The next day Carol, on her way to work, went to drop the kids off at the babysitter's home. She saw John's van around the corner. He was waiting for her. To avoid him, she went down the side street. But he came up right behind her and tried to run her off the road. He forced her into a bank parking lot and blocked her in so she couldn't move the car. John said he wanted to talk to her. She opened the window just a crack for fear that John would attack her.

John said that he was sorry. He was crying and asked how he could fix their situation. He swore that he would never hurt her again. He said, "I just don't want you to see this other guy". She told John that their relationship was over. He asked if they could talk about it. She said, "I just don't want you to see this other guy". She told John that their relationship was over. He asked if they could talk about it. She said "No. It's over". It took over an hour before John would let her out of the parking lot.

The next day she filed a personal protection order (PPO) against him. She said that the P.P.O didn't cost her anything. It just took a little time. As soon as she filed, he pulled around the corner from where she was.

That same day, while Carol was at work, John broke into her house. He went in through the upstairs window. It was a very warm day – over 90 degrees. He cut the ceiling fan. He also cut the cords on the air conditioner and cut the refrigerator cord so it wouldn't get cold. Everything looked like it was running, but when she went to use it, it wouldn't work.

John also took all the birth certificates and legal papers showing that she had custody of the kids. Carol called John's mother to confront him and to try to get the papers back, but he denied doing it.

Eventually John was arrested and charged with stalking. Carol didn't hear from John until he called from jail on their son's birthday. John's mother called everyday, pleading for Carol to drop the charges. One of John's girlfriends even showed up with a tape recorder wanting to tape their conversation while she asked Carol to drop the charges. Carol said she wouldn't drop the stalking charges because of all that John had done to her. The girlfriend didn't know about all the violence, so Carol informed her. The girlfriend realized John had been lying to her also.

6

dad. When he was released, Carol let her son see his dad. However, when she went to pick the son up, John wouldn't leave the side of her car. Carol went to get John's mother to see if she could get him to leave the side of the car. John said something to his mother, but Carol didn't hear it. John wanted to go to Carol's house, but she said her boyfriend was there. He said "Oh" and had a very sinister look on his face. He was very angry when she drove away.

Carol got home and was talking to her boyfriend when they heard a noise on the front porch. Her boyfriend looked out the window and said, "John's on the way in!"

John kicked the front door in and immediately kicked the bedroom door in. As Carol's boyfriend turned around, John shot him in the chest without saying a word.

John was wearing hunting clothes. He turned the gun on her and said "You're gonna die – bitch!" Then he shot her. The bullet went through her chest and exploded in her stomach. At the time he shot her, Carol wasn't scared anymore until he looked at her and said "Look at your boyfriend, doesn't he look good dead?"

Then he said "You're gonna watch me die." He came down on her head with the butt of the rifle, injuring her head and hand. The gun handle broke on her leg. Because she was already shot she didn't feel anything. She just saw the pieces fly off the butt of the gun. He screamed at her to look at him and when she did, he had the barrel of the gun under his chin. She put her hand on the side of her face and turned her head. He pulled the trigger. Carol heard the gun go off and she could see "things" flying over her head. Then she heard him hit the floor.

All this time, her baby was in the crib and had seen the whole thing. When Carol heard John hit the floor, she stood up and wrapped herself with a blanket and tried to pick up the baby-she couldn't. She walked out of the room to get help. She had to leave the baby in the bedroom with the two dead bodies. Carol went into the living room and picked up the phone. She was unable to get a dial tone – the phone lines had been cut.

John had been outside that night since 10:00 p.m. and it was now 12:30 a.m. Obviously, he had planned this out and had plenty of time to decide against this course of action. "In fact, the majority of husbands who kill their wives stalk them first, and far from the "crime of passion" that it's so often called, killing a wife is usually a decision, not a loss of control. Those men who are the most violent are not all carried away by fury. In fact, their heart rates actually drop and they become physiologically calmer as they become more violent." [1]

John had cut the phone lines. He had watched the house, sitting in his van across the street. He had been drinking. Some stalkers may become involved with alcohol or substance abuse. It helps to fuel their behavior. Ultimately their behavior reflects their desperation to hold on to the relationship.

Neither Carol nor her boyfriend had noticed him outside. One of the neighbors thought she saw John but didn't call the police because she wasn't sure it was him. He had been outside watching the house for two hours.

When Carol went to the phone and found it was dead, she woke up her son who was sleeping. Surprisingly, he hadn't heard anything. She said "Tommy you got to get up and help Mom". He asked, "Why"?. "It hurt her so much to tell him why he had to get up. She said, "Because Daddy shot me."

Tommy was afraid to go out of the house. He said, "I can't go out there". She said, "Well if you can't go out there we'll go out together". So she wrapped the blanket around herself and stood up one more time and they walked out of the house. They went down the steps and to the edge of the yard. She said, "Tommy you have to help Mom". He went and banged on the neighbor's door. By this time the neighbor had already called the police. Carol had made it up to the porch. The neighbor wanted Carol to come into the house, but she stayed on the porch because she was afraid she'd get blood on their floor.

Carol sat on the porch and waited for the police. All she was worried about was getting her baby out of the house. She kept saying, "Get my baby out". About ten minutes later she saw the police carrying her baby out of the house. That's all Carol cared about. She was put in an ambulance and taken to the hospital.

Carol always feared John, but never thought that John would have done anything this violent. He made a lot of threats but he never followed through on them. Obviously she misjudged him. She didn't think he was so serious. She didn't realize he was that close to the edge. She knew John was violent but she didn't think he was capable of murder. She thought John felt threatened when she found someone wasn't his anymore he figured he had nothing else to live for. To this day Carol wonders why John didn't just go out to a field and kill himself and leave everyone else alone. But she reasoned that he had to go out with a bang. That's the way he was. Once he shot her boyfriend and knew he was dead, John knew he'd go to prison for life, so he might as well just kill himself and take everyone out with him. John didn't think of anyone except himself. He didn't think about the kids or how they'd be.

Carol feels the kids are better off without a father like John. It hurts her to see them without a father, but eventually she'll find someone who could be their father.

At least now, Carol feels she has a chance. She says: "I don't have to look behind me. My kids don't have to see their Mom get hit. They don't have to look behind us in the car anymore and say 'Mom, Dad's back there.' They don't have to worry about that anymore." Carol's son is embarrassed that his Dad killed someone and shot his mother. He says, "I don't have a Dad". He won't say how his Dad died. He has a hard time telling people that. He just says his Dad is gone.

John was very controlling. This is a common characteristic among stalkers. He didn't like Carol's family because they took her time and attention from him. Everything needed to be for him. If it didn't go his way, John would get violent. One time, while she was pregnant with their son, he woke her at 4 a.m. and started pounding on her face because she forgot to wake him. He said he had things to do. The times he wasn't physically violent, he was verbally abusive. The verbal attacks were always there. He'd say things like, "You're so fat, you could never find someone else."

10

Even when he was in jail, John was controlling. He'd call her on the phone and say, "I'll call you at 9 a.m. You better be there". She'd hang up, and he'd call again. She'd take the phone off the hook. Whenever she placed the phone back on the hook, he would call again. He tried to control her over the phone.

Whenever Carol tried to show some independence, the stalking escalated. He needed to know that he had not lost control over her. When she found someone else, he couldn't accept it. He couldn't accept someone else in his place and being 'Daddy' to his kids.

Following the shooting, Carol had five surgeries while she was in the hospital and has had two more since. She has an opening on her side, scar tissue down the front of her body and she lost ½ of her left breast. She is very self-conscious about her body. She's not looking for a relationship because she doesn't know how she'd deal with exposing her injuries.

She wouldn't let the kids move back into the house. Their experiences had an impact on them. Her son wets the bed, starts fires and has problems in school. He is being tested for emotional stability. Her youngest daughter is very clingy. She talks about the blood that flew over her head. She is four years old and still wants a pacifier; she has to have something to calm her down. She says "Mom I want a new Daddy real bad" It breaks Carol's heart to hear that. The daughter knows that 'Daddy' wasn't a good guy, but she still loved him. Carol tells her daughter it's all right to love him even though you don't like what he did.

Carol thinks that the stalking laws can work, but the police need to get more information on how to deal with the problem. She said,

11

Carol thinks that the stalking laws can work, but the police need to get more information on how to deal with the problem. She said, "The problem has always been there, they just have to learn how to deal with it".

To those who are in similar situations, Carol says you need to find a way out. There are safe houses you can go to. Carol said she would never have gone to a safe house, but now realizes it would have been a good idea. She said she didn't want to leave her things because he would have ruined them. But now she says that possessions aren't that important in life. She also said, "If they threaten to kill you, take that threat seriously. Don't ever think that they are not serious. I never thought John was serious. It escalated to the point of all the violence and murder. Take it serious. If he threatens to kill you get out of there, he will do something."

Carol said she now understands that what happened on that fateful day was just a matter of time - because he was that controlling. Even if he went to jail 2 or 3 years more for stalking, when he got out something still would have happened. Because that's the way he was.

When asked her how she survived through all of this, Carol said, "For my kids, I have to for my kids. When I was sitting there after he shot me, I felt I had to get up and help my kids. I didn't care about me. I knew they needed a Mother. I didn't think I was going to die. I never once thought I was going to die. I thought I was going to live through this. I was worried about who was going to take care of the kids. I felt I had to get through it for the kids, the kids needed me. Every day I get out of bed knowing I have to feed them. I have to put clothes on their back and pay these bills so we can live where we're living. I try to make a better life for us. I didn't move them back into the house where they had all those bad memories. They each have their own bedrooms and have everything they didn't have back then. I hope it'll help them. I try to live every day and take care of them."

Carol was laying in the hospital right after she got shot, when the Detective handling the case came in. The detective sent her family out of the room. He looked at her and said "Well, are you happy now? Did you see what you did?" the detective was referring to the fact that she had eventually dropped the charges against John, because their son had been upset.

When she looked up at him, she said, "I'm sorry." He said, "It's a little late for that now isn't it?" and he just walked out of the room. Carol doesn't know if he took the murder personally. She says, "They have to see that there are violent people out there and they cannot blame the victim. The victim had nothing to do with it. I did not choose to get shot. I didn't choose for my boyfriend to die and I didn't choose for John to kill himself. You can't blame the victim. You blame the person who did the killing - and no one else."

Carol considers herself lucky, her stalker is gone.

Chapter One

STALKING BASICS

Can you imagine experiencing what Carol went through? Can you imagine being afraid to answer the phone, open a letter or go to the store? Many stalking victims are afraid to do these simple things. As you read this book, many are going through similar circumstances. Stalking victims live with fear every day of their lives.

Carol's situation was typical of many stalking cases. Her stalking took the form of abuse, vandalism, threats and ultimately murder. Carol was stalked for eight years prior to this tragic conclusion. When she told me her story, I just couldn't believe that she could so calmly tell me about what happened. In a few months she was going to go through yet another surgery to help close up the hole on her side. The only time she broke down and cried was when she told me about her son and his strength in going to get her help. Carol's story revealed an inner strength in that she overcame her misfortune and continued to build a life for her family. Unfortunately, her story repeats the same gruesome facts that hundreds of victims share every day.

As for myself, I had never heard of the term *stalking* until I started teaching. Because my courses dealt with security measures, students in my classes, told me about how they were being stalked or how someone they knew was being stalked. It was brought to my attention so often, I started researching it.

The first case of stalking I researched dealt with an attractive blonde female approximately thirty five years old. She had two children. She lived in a nice home with curtains on all of her windows except those around the back door. One day, she started getting calls and notes from someone she didn't know. It gave her the "creeps", but she wasn't too concerned. However, it just wouldn't stop.

One evening when she was out and her children were home, someone started banging on her door. This unknown person went from door to door and rattled the doorknobs. The children were scared out of their minds. When she got home she called the police, but since she didn't know who was doing it and didn't have a description of the person, the police couldn't do much. She told her neighbors about what was going on and asked them to keep an eye out for her. She was terrified for her children.

This harassment continued for approximately two years. The idea of getting a gun was abandoned, simply because of her kids. Then one night about 2:00 a.m., a neighbor saw someone placing something on the front windshield of her car. The neighbor went out and caught the stalker. The police were called. The stalker was a man she didn't know, but she discovered that the guy would walk around neighborhoods at night looking into windows. This is the technique he used on her. He looked into her back window. She pressed charges against the stalker.

However, the ordeal did not end there. One evening the stalker's wife visited her, begging for both her husband's release and for the charges to be dropped. The victim refused. He terrorized her and her family for two years! The wife said that the stalker didn't mean any harm. The victim wasn't buying it. She asked the wife if she knew of the stalker's behavior. The wife said she didn't. The victim asked where did she think the stalker went when he left their home in the middle of the night. The wife said she worked days so she always went to bed early. When he left, he would say that he was going out for cigarettes!

The more I researched, the more I discovered what a devastating crime stalking is. It can debilitate both victim and family with shocking force. I also discovered that people really don't know what stalking is. Because of this, I decided to do a documentary on stalking in conjunction with Comcast Cablevision of Garden City, Michigan. Once I started looking for individuals who had been stalked, my phone never stopped ringing with horrendous stories, like Carol's. Most of the cases had similar elements to them: the victims experienced being attracted to someone charming, whose flattery made them "feel special"; then came the harrowing phone calls, vandalism, threats and repentance that is characteristic of stalking cases.

However, many of us aren't quite sure what stalking is. When someone is asked to define it, a common response may be, "It's someone following another person" or "It's someone who continually calls another person." We have an idea that it may be threatening in some way, but we don't understand the full dynamics of it. Carol's case illustrates what can happen at the beginning, middle and end of many stalking cases.

Today, there are numerous accounts of stalking cases. "Survey findings indicate that stalking is a bigger problem than previously thought, effecting about 1.4 million victims annually." [2] Also, it has been estimated, that approximately 1,000,000 women and 400,000 men are stalked in the United States each year.

Though, many people think stalking is a new crime, it's not. The fact is, stalking has been around as long as people have interacted with one another. Its "newness" is that it is now being classified as a crime; whereas, it once was classified under domestic violence, trespassing or harassment. Still today, some police departments are classifying them under these areas.

In our society, many of us never think anything bad will ever happen to us. We think that when bad things do happen, they happen to other people in other cities. The fact is that, *you* could be stalked and hurt by a stalker. Look at Carol's case. Even though she was threatened, she never really thought that her stalker would attempt to commit murder. He made a lot of threats, but never followed through. Until the final act.

When Carol was first being stalked, there were no anti-stalking laws in existence. Now we have anti-stalking laws to help stalking victims. The definitions vary by state, but the basic concepts are similar. Stalking is the continued or repeated harassment of an individual, which would cause the individual to be concerned for their personal safety. "States statues typically define stalking, in essence, as culpable and repeated following and harassment of another person. Many States require that the stalker exhibit a pattern of conduct and possess an intent to instill fear in the victim."[3]

Harassment of an individual means "To trouble or pursue relentlessly with cares, annoyances, etc.; torment".[4] Carol's stalker started out by being someone with whom she shared her life with. Then, as she tried to break off the relationship, he continually and repeatedly harassed her. He followed her, ran her off the road, vandalized her home, threatened her, all of which caused her to be very concerned about her

17

safety.

Stalking victims are not only harassed by their stalkers, they can be terrorized by them. Frustrating both victims and the police, stalkers can terrorize their victims without breaking the law. Many types of stalking behavior is still considered legal.

This can be seen in the Jane McAllister story. For eighteen months her stalker followed her, told her he loved her, offered her marriage and called her. After going to the authorities, Jane discovered her stalker had both a police and psychiatric record. The latter notation was demonstrated by his persistent aggression, which was highlighted when he attempted to hit her with his car while she was walking with a male companion.

Angered over her stalker's craziness, Jane asked the police for help and was told to dial 911, if he continued his pursuits. Seeing him lurking in a neighbor's yard, Jane dialed the number, but she was refused help because the stalker was on another person's property, not hers! She was also advised that witnesses had to corroborate her complaints about her stalker's gambits. For months Jane anxiously and fearfully expected her stalker to do something violent. Uncannily breaking no laws, the stalker succeeded in "breaking" Jane's life, while the police helplessly waited until an overt assault happened. "The police were not insensitive, but they were stymied." [5] The stalker had broken no laws, but managed to violate almost all aspects of her life. The police tried to be helpful, but they said they couldn't do anything until he actually assaulted her.

Jane was terrified and suffered a range of emotions. She quotes, "Though he was free to move about, I was living in a state of siege".[6]

Doing what she could to help others, Jane began a support group. She enlightened the participants about stalking and its legal entanglements, which made the police ineffective, until the commission of an actual crime against the victim occurred. In many cases, for a variety of reasons, police still don't do as much as the victim may want.

Stalking involves a series of actions - not just a single act. Viewed in isolation, a single stalking act may be perfectly legal behavior. For example, writing love notes, sending flowers, calling someone on the phone, are not illegal. If anything, at first glance, these actions are seen as complimentary and positive in nature. In Carol's situation, when her stalker wanted to know where she went, what time she'd be back, and proceeded to follow her around, she was flattered. To her it was a demonstration of affection. In reality, these were warning signs of potentially aggressive behavior, but she didn't see it that way.

Later, when she wanted to end their relationship, he still followed and called her. His actions took on another meaning. His charm changed into possessiveness. All of a sudden the same actions that impressed her, began to terrorize her. When actions are intended to cause fear or injury, they form a pattern of conduct that is considered illegal.

An important aspect of stalking involves criminal intent. In most states, in order to convict a stalker, it must be demonstrated that the stalker show criminal intent to cause fear in the victim. "The conduct of the stalker must be "willful," "purposeful", "intentional", or "knowing"[7] There is no doubt, that these criteria were met in Carol's case. If the victim is reasonably frightened by the stalker's behavior, then the intent aspect of the crime has been met in these states.

It is difficult to prove that someone is purposely causing you fear and alarm when they're sending you flowers and stating their love for you. However, in some states, proof that the stalker intended to cause fear is not necessary. "Many states do not require proof that the defendant intended to cause fear as long as he intended to commit the act that resulted in fear". [8]

Threatening behavior is another aspect of stalking. In most states, the stalker must pose a threat or behave in a way that causes a reasonable person to feel threatened. Many stalkers don't physically attack, but the threat of violence is still there. Victims of stalking can never let their guard down. Even if victims aren't physically harmed, they suffer tremendously. They suffer anxiety, great fear and complete disruption of their lives. Because the threat is implied to the victim, other people initially may not see what the victim sees in the problem.

Carol felt threatened when John cut the cords on her appliances. If you considered just this action, without knowing the whole story, it may not seem like a threatening act. However, Carol knew that "these little annoyances" were part of a larger device to scare her into submission.

John behaved in a threatening manner verbally and physically. Most states have provisions that acknowledge that stalking occurs when a reasonable person would feel threatened, even if the victim had not been threatened verbally or in writing. "Under the statutes, the threat need not be written or verbal to instill fear (for example, a stalker can convey a threat by sending the victim black roses, forming his hand into a gun and pointing it at her, or delivering a dead animal to her doorstep)." [9]

One stalker tied a black ribbon around the neck of the victim's dog. As we will see later, he was communicating to his victim that he could get to her *anywhere*. The exact threat requirement varies by state. In fourteen states if the stalker simply makes a threat against the victim, he can be charged with the crime of stalking.

ARE ALL STALKERS INSANE?

When we think of stalking, we would like to think that the stalker is an "insane" person, who doesn't know right from wrong. "While some stalkers suffer from mental disabilities, the majority of them are perfectly sane."[10] Some stalkers have personality disorders. Others display some form of mental illness such as schizophrenia or paranoia. Stalkers can also display delusional disorders, while others display obsessive behaviors. According to Funk and Wagnalls Encyclopedia, to obsess means 'to occupy or trouble the mind to an excessive degree; preoccupy; harass; haunt.' [11]

We can see this in Carol's case; she occupied John's mind. She says that her stalker had made her his life. When she was no longer available for him, the stalker, sensing that there was nothing else for him, contemplated death. He haunted her when he was alive. Now that he's dead, memories of his violence still haunt her. It's what he wanted: to be in her life, forever.

STALKING SITUATIONS

Stalking situations may involve celebrities, co-workers, casual acquaintances, or strangers.

We are familiar with celebrity stalking because of media attention. Movies, television, radio and magazines bring our favorite stars a little closer to us. When we hear or read about a *star*, we may imagine that we know them. Some of us may fantasize about the person in question, but that is all. It's all in the imaginative scope of entertainment. This however, is not the case for celebrity stalkers. In some celebrity stalking cases, the stalker, having a delusion termed erotomania (wherein the stalker believes that the celebrity actually loves him in return), seeks out the "object of desire", regardless of circumstance. Some of us may think that being stalked is just a risk that goes along with being famous; that celebrity stalking "goes with the territory". However, we should all be able to feel safe as we go through or daily lives.

Many celebrities have been stalked, or are currently being stalked including TV personalities, sports heroes and local celebrities. Cher, Vanna White, David Letterman (his stalker eventually committed suicide by kneeling in front of a moving train) and many others, are hailed by fans and given traditional gifts. The gifts range from flowers, fan letters, stuffed animals, to the bizarre and repulsive, such as a syringe of blood or even human body parts.

Being a celebrity and being in the limelight has both advantages and disadvantages. The advantage is having loving and adoring fans and the disadvantage is of a fan crossing the line-to the point of danger and death. One celebrity stalking case that turned deadly was the Rebecca Schaefer murder. On July 18, 1989, she was shot in the chest, with a .357 magnum, by her stalker, Robert Bardo.

Rebecca was the star of a sitcom called *My Sister Sam*. Robert Bardo saw her, became obsessed, and stalked her for two years prior to killing her. Twice he went to Warner Bros. Studios to see her, but was turned away by security personnel. Having written the actress for an autographed photo, Bardo felt that the picture sent to him was a

22

token of love.

Getting no further contact and psychotically feeling betrayed, especially after Schaefer portrayed a 'promiscuous' role in a movie-he wanted to kill her. Finding her dwelling, he went to the door. When she answered, he grabbed her arm and shot-killing her.

The murder unearthed a plethora of national stalking testimonies from ordinary people. As more people came out and told of their horrendous stories, it indicated what a problem stalking is in our country.

Co-worker stalkings are not unusual. Being safe at work is something we shouldn't have to be concerned about. However, many people don't feel safe at work because they are being stalked there.

Victims can be stalked by someone who is not an employee or they can be stalked by a co-worker. Unless victims quit their jobs, the possibility of seeing their stalker every day at a place where they expect to be safe, is very high. It can be terrifying, frightening and frustrating when all they want to do is take care of their family, themselves and do a good job.

When someone is being stalked by a co-worker, the stalker knows where the victim will be most of the day. It's an ideal situation for the stalker. At first the victim may not even know who the stalker is. One day the victim may receive a rose at her/his desk or a small box of chocolates. The victim might even be flattered, at first. When it's discovered who it is, and appreciation is expressed, the stalker may feel encouraged to continue. When the victim tries to explain that she/he is not interested, what was once flattering attention may turn ominous.

Recently, a stalking situation occurred in a company in the Midwest, where a female was being stalked by a male co-worker. The victim had a boyfriend who also worked at the company. The stalker was small in stature and appeared meek and mild at first glance. He left the victim various gifts such as perfume, flowers, love letters, cards and jewelry. The letters he sent to her contained words of love and affection and some had a religious tone to them. Some of the gifts were expensive. In the winter, he cleaned the snow from her windshield. The victim told him she was not interested in him. She thought that since the stalker knew her boyfriend, he'd leave her alone. He didn't.

She told her supervisor who down played the situation. This made her very angry because she thought she had a very good reputation and should be taken seriously. Unfortunately, she wasn't.

The stalker was close to retirement and the victim didn't want him fired. She just wanted to be left alone. When other employees told the stalker to leave the victim alone, surprisingly, this meek and mild man turned on them, telling them to mind their own business. When the victim's boyfriend confronted the stalker at work, the stalker turned on him viciously, and told the boyfriend that he didn't deserve the victim. That the boyfriend was much larger than the stalker didn't deter him at *all*.

This went on for more than a year. The victim was getting more and more concerned for her safety. She couldn't escape the stalker at work because he was assigned to a location near her. Her supervisor kept minimizing the situation while other workers cautioned the woman that management was fearful of firing him, because of the revenge that he might take; namely, returning to shoot his "enemies".

The victim was at her wits end. She hated going into work and hated that she wasn't being helped. Eventually, she had to take time off of work because of an unrelated illness. When she was recuperating she was extremely stressed out by the idea of having to go back to that intolerable situation. The stress was not helping her condition. Then one evening, while convalescing at home, she received a phone call from work. The stalker had died at work from what appeared to be a heart attack. Ambivalent feelings rushed over her. She hadn't wanted his death, yet she was relieved that he was gone.

If someone is being stalked at work, they need to tell their employer about the situation, for their own safety. This way, calls or visitors can be screened before there is contact with the victim. Unfortunately, this situation can be extremely embarrassing for the victim especially if the employer is uncaring and also blames the victim. A co-worker stalking is intolerable if you have a concerned employer; if the employer can't be bothered with your concerns, the situation intensifies.

Not only can someone be stalked by a co-worker, but people can also be stalked by an intimate friend or partner while they are at work. How could this happen? Aren't we safe at work? "Each year between 1992 and 1996, more than 2 million U.S. residents were victims of a violent crime while they were at work or on duty." [12]

One victim was fired because her stalker kept showing up at her work. She worked in a beauty salon and her boss was concerned that the stalker was scaring away clients. The stalker would stand outside the picture window and stare at the victim. So now the victim lives in fear *and* doesn't have a job to support herself.

When a victim is stalked at work, it often takes its toll on the victim's outlook of others. One victim, who had been stalked for 8 years, stated that she is very careful whom she talks to and what she says to anyone. Her life was in such turmoil, that extreme care was given even in routine chats with people, in fear that an innocent remark may be taken the wrong way.

Casual acquaintance stalking is another form of stalking. This type of stalking often begins very innocently. For instance, Sue meets Tom at a party. They become friends and exchange phone numbers, or the stalker finds hers in the telephone directory. Tom then calls Sue for a date, but she declines, for one reason or another. Most of us have experienced similar situations. We may be uncomfortable about telling people that we are not interested in them and we hope they go away. Many people would just forget about Sue, but not Tom. He does not take "No" for an answer. Many stalkers don't just go away.

An example of a casual acquaintance stalking happened to a criminal justice student. This female student was being pursued by her male classmate. The stalker would show his interest at first, by asking the student out and trying to talk to her during class breaks. However, his actions became extreme. He would call her home up to 27 times a day. She told him she was not interested in dating him, but he couldn't be dissuaded. The harassment got to the point that when the class broke for break, she would surround herself with her friends in the hope of discouraging the stalker. He was persistent however, pulling her away from her friends and suggesting that they go to his car where he would show her his guns.

26

Soon, she never went anywhere without a male companion with her, because she was concerned about her safety. She didn't go to the police, because she did not want to aggravate the situation. Physically, she didn't feel threatened by him, because he was smaller then she was (This is a false security, in that size means nothing if the stalker wants to abuse a victim!). Eventually the class ended, and the stalking stopped. Unbelievably, the stalker was hired by a local police department!

Another category of stalking is *stranger stalking*. Stranger stalkings are terrifying because the victim doesn't know who the culprit is. Being stalked by someone you know is bad enough, but a "faceless foe" is worse. Everyday business is marred by the thought that the stalker is always near by, perhaps as close as a breath.

The most common stalking situations are *domestic violence stalkings*. They are very dangerous because the individuals have known each other intimately. The stalker knows what the victim fears the most. The stalker learns the secrets of the victim, and, subsequently, plays them against her.

All stalking situations need to be taken seriously. In certain cases, the stalkers seem to be flattering and attentive to the victim, but these can be signals of trouble ahead. Someone looking in from the outside, would never consider such a situation to be potentially dangerous. But stalking cases can escalate from a seemingly innocent situation to a violent and deadly one.

Stalking incidents often end with violence for women. Violence against women is not new in our society. Its consequences effect everyone, families, children and our society in general. Carol's example proves the physical and emotional damage. She and her children are scarred, physically and emotionally. They will never forget what they went through. There are many families experiencing such tribulation. However, there is more social and legal awareness now concerning violence against women. There is a legislative act called, The Violence Against Women Act, Title IV of the Violence Crime Control and Enforcement Act of 1994. This act depicts our nation's concern and efforts to end the violence against women. The National Institute of Justice, in response to the Act, is conducting a research and evaluation program to gather knowledge about responses to violence against women. One case that started with violence then turned into a stalking situation was Mary's case...

STALKING CASE: TWO

"You will never leave me and if you do, as long as you live and breath, I'll never be out of your life."

Mary had been married to Joe for 6 years. During her marriage he had been very abusive. When she separated from him he would show up at her work. He would bring her gifts of reconciliation: notes and gourmet food, all designed to get her back. He would follow her by car. He would appear at public places, friends' homes and even her parents' home. There was no place to really get away from him. He was affecting her life, work and her family's lives. His behavior included assaulting her friends and waking her parents up in the middle of the night in drunken rages. Joe affected every aspect of her life; 24 hours a day, 7 days a week.

Mary had good reason to fear her husband, who had abused her at home, been unfaithful to her-though he mockingly accused her of having affairs-and had threatened her life. He would also call her names. One time he pulled out a shotgun, pointed it at her and said, "I'm going to kill you". She would receive phone calls from him, telling her that she needed to be looking over her shoulder.

Several friends and co-workers were assaulted by Joe, for either trying to help Mary or attempting to speak to her. Even if a person told Joe that he had seen Mary, Joe would go into a jealous rage against the person, whom he mused as her lover.

One night Joe was hiding in her car. When she came out of a bowling alley and got into her car and took off, he sat up in the back seat. She was scared to death. She knew she was in trouble one way or another. She didn't know if he had a weapon but he had threatened her life several times. At that point all she wanted to do was keep the situation from escalating and just go with whatever he said. "Let's talk", she nervously suggested. By this time Joe was crying, and saying "I can't believe you left me, why don't you love me anymore, I'll never do anything to you, don't you believe that?" They drove through town and he told her to pull behind a store and they'd discuss what was happening. As she told him that she needed to go on with her life, he began to get angry. He slapped her a couple of times and grabbed her by the hair. It escalated from abuse to rape.

Joe had raped her on a couple of other occasions when they were married. But she did not consider that such a dreadful attack would occur this time. She thought if she sat and talked and told him what he wanted to hear she could drop him off, go home and just get out of the situation. She didn't expect it to escalate to the point of terror. It did.

On another occasion, after she left him, he broke her nose. He asked her to meet with him, and she agreed. While driving down the road, Joe was questioning her and asking her things about her life. She was honest with him. He accused her of having an affair with one of her co-workers. He kept accusing her. She told him that what she does with her life now had nothing to do with him; that it was her life. He then backhanded her. She knew immediately that her nose was broken. Blood flowed down the front of her shirt. She went to the emergency room of a nearby hospital, where it was confirmed that her nose was broken and that she'd have to have surgery. She was mortified. She had left him and was beginning to make it on her own, when this nightmare had to resurrect itself! She couldn't believe she let this happen.

She was so embarrassed about what happened she didn't want anyone to know she had met him. So she had lied about where she went. To explain her condition, she said that a car ran through a red light, she slammed on her brakes and hit her face on the steering wheel.

She agreed to meet him because he had *persisted* so much about meeting with her that exhaustion set in; she couldn't take it anymore. She met him because not talking to him wasn't working and the police weren't doing anything. She thought that perhaps one final talk would settle all this once and for all. They were supposed to go to a nearby family restaurant and straighten this out. She was sure that she could convince him that it was over; that this was it. Her life was moving on and the divorce was moving on. He had tried to commit suicide right after she filed for divorce so she backed off a little. She filed for divorce in April of 1987, but it was not final until 1989. She didn't want his death on her hands. If he had killed himself in 1987 there'd be no doubt in her mind that it was her fault, because she was leaving him. Today, she knows if he was going to do it, there would be nothing she could do to stop it. She understands now, that we all make our own personal decisions.

She filed a personal protection order because she had a domestic restraining order that was activated on the date of the divorce in 1987, but wasn't getting the backing from police. She knew about PPO's because she had worked in a domestic violence shelter and was involved in the enactment of PPO's prior to them being available. Thinking that this would help her better in getting police to enforce

31

it, she obtained one.

She thought the PPO would also prevent Joe from taking her daughter from school. She learned a frustrating lesson. To her, the P.P.O seemed very specific. Part of the PPO options involved minor children. On the application was a box pertaining to any children in common. She checked that box, thinking that this would prevent him from taking their child from anywhere. Because of the PPO, Mary and Joe had worked out very specific rules about removing a minor child except during a custody exchange.

A few months after obtaining the PPO in April, Joe tried to abduct their daughter from school. The principal knew about the PPO and Mary brought a picture of Joe to the school, so they would recognize him. The principal was walking down the hall and saw Joe wandering around the school looking for their daughter. Mary called the police. She explained about PPO options involving children. The police said that, yes, she marked the box removing the minor child but she didn't list the name of the school. So they couldn't do anything about it. When she applied for it again, she was very specific. She was encouraged to write on the PPO that a minor child could not be removed from anywhere except during custody exchange points.

While Mary was being stalked, she went to the police on numerous occasions. They minimized her situation as ex-spouses who could not get along. One sergeant from her local police department told her that they were two people involved in a "urinating" contest. They considered her situation as just another domestic dispute. She now knows that some police officers are helpful, but she was speaking from her experiences and interaction with police officers in her area. She thought that at the time, they were very victimizing. She thought that they minimized the PPO's and minimized domestic issues.

Many women have requested protection from law enforcement officers. Some have received help and protection and some haven't. Even in situations where protection is given, there is no guarantee that the stalking will stop. Carol had called the police and filed a personal protection order and her stalking did not stop. Over time it escalated. "Studies in Detroit and Kansas City reveal that 90 percent of all those murdered by their intimate partners called police at least once; more than half had called five times or more" [13]

At first, Mary didn't receive the help and protection that she needed. She explained that one time while speaking to two deputies, one said they had chronic women callers. That they are constantly called to certain houses to settle domestic disputes. Sometimes when these women call, they'll stop at the store and get a pop and chips because by the time they get to the caller's home, it's either settled down and they're making up or one has left. That way they don't have to get involved. This was before the law was enacted. Now the police have to arrest the offender.

Mary couldn't believe the unprofessional conduct that she often experienced with law enforcement. Even though there were numerous documented violations of PPO's and she had tape recordings of phone calls, the police didn't do a lot to help her. The Annoying Calls Bureau from the phone company put a tap on her phone and she had caller ID. The sergeant in charge said his interpretation of the stalking law read that he needed to be present while the phone call was being made by the stalker in order for him to act. She knew this couldn't be true because not everyone lives with a police officer. She asked him, "Do you want to move in with me and wait till he calls and then you can act"? She thought it was a ridiculous comment for him to make. He said that was how he interpreted it and that was how he was going to act when she claimed the PPO was being violated.

Mary started documenting her stalking incidents on the advice of one police officer that was very encouraging. He told her to document phone calls, and keep a log. He told her a law had passed where she could tape record the conversations. He explained that as long as one party involved in a conversation was aware that it was being taped, that it was legal to do so and that these tapes would be admissible in court. She did that and had several tapes of her stalker threatening her and threatening her new husband. In one series of calls, the "caller" phoned twelve times in one hour! The police advised her to unplug her phone. However, Mary felt very strongly that she shouldn't have to make those concessions in her life because *he's* doing this to *her*. Why should she unplug her phone when he's threatening her? He should be the one facing consequences for his actions. Eventually it got out of hand and she said that's it and unplugged the phone. However, before doing so, she would call the police and say, "He just called, I don't want you to come to my house, all I want you to do is file a complaint, just document this." She felt if the police were documenting it also, that it would be more power in case she had to go to court.

Mary didn't start documenting the stalking incidences at the beginning because she wasn't aware how helpful a log could prove to be later. When these incidences were occurring, her assumption was that she'd call the police and there would be a record of it somewhere. She found out later that the police only kept records for a short period of time. If no charges were filed, the reports were thrown out and there would no longer be any existing copies. No records, no file, no arrest! When she left for good, Mary had 150 police reports from being stalked by him. With a dresser full of documentation, she still records all evidence about her stalker.

When Mary did go to court, the judge would not allow her to admit the tapes she had. The "taped evidence" proved to be useless. When she had her day in court, the judge would not accept the three-to-four hours worth of evidence, inasmuch as she surmised that they might have been "doctored up".

To this day Mary is unsure if her stalker ever loved her. She thinks that she was more of a possession. He saw her as something to be gotten, to be had, to be controlled. This quote gives insight into the motives of the stalker: "The typical female victim thought she had been stalked because her assailant wanted to control, scare, or keep her in a relationship. About 60 % of stalking by intimate partners started before a relationship ended. Men reported intimidation and control as possible stalker motivations."[14]

Mary's stalker refused to forget her; he refused to lose the control he had. He said to her, "You'll never leave me and if you do, as long as you live and breath I'll never be out of your life. You'll have to deal with me until the day you die however long that may be." It's been true. He has never been out of her life. They have been divorced for 8 years. His primary control mechanism is their child. He uses their child as an excuse to call, as an excuse to be in the area and to be able to get at her. All of his issues are still about her. The target is always her..her..her.

Even Mary's new husband was assaulted. They were married in April 1989; in July of 1989 Joe had visitation with the daughter for the weekend. He brought the daughter to her grandparents' home, where the family was enjoying a barbecue on the fourth of July. Joe dropped the daughter off. But he could not leave without making insulting remarks to Mary's new husband or inappropriate remarks about her. Remarks concerning if she was doing things with the new husband that she had done with him. Joe was trying to let him know that she had been with someone else besides him. He wanted to see if he could provoke a response.

Joe dropped the daughter off and the husband picked the daughter up and Joe said to the husband, "How does it feel that you have to deal with me until she turns 18"? At this time she was 2 ½ . Mary's husband replied, "I'll do whatever I have to do if that's what it takes". Joe pulled out of the driveway and made some other sarcastic comment that no one heard. The husband went to set the daughter down. The daughter went around the corner of the house and the next thing they knew, Joe was on the husband's back punching him! They fell to the ground. The two were rolling around on the ground. Her husband was trying to get a hold of him to stop. Joe kept punching and punching. The husband fell into a lawn mover. He was cut pretty bad.

Mary's dad and brother, who were in the garage, intervened. Her dad was standing over Joe with a shovel. He had grabbed the shovel and was ready to pound away. However, Mary's father resisted, because he could have seriously hurt Joe and he didn't think Joe was worth going to jail for.

The police were called and a report was filed. Joe went to the police station and filed a counter report saying that it was self-defense! He said that *his* father, who was not even at the event, had witnessed the whole thing.

Mary pressed charges and Joe plead guilty. He was fined, ordered to intensive outpatient psychiatric counseling, placed on one year probation, and was ordered not have any contact with her or her husband-ever.

Joe ended up going to jail because he refused counseling. He served three nights in jail. The courts basically said, if you go to jail for three nights, you don't have to go to counseling. That's what Joe did.

The stalking put a lot of strain and stress on Mary's new marriage. It's been extremely frustrating for her new husband to not be able to do anything for her. She sees him struggling with the fact that there's nothing he can do. He is helpless to stop Joe from troubling them. He's by her side at every court date, every conversation with police and with everything she has been through. He is frustrated with what's going on with their daughter. The daughter is now in counseling with what has happened. He's frustrated with everything that Joe has done, and that the system still allows Joe to roam about the family with impunity! Mary's husband doesn't think that Joe should breath the same air that she and her daughter breath because of everything that has happened.

Mary has gone to court several times because her stalker violated the conditions of the PPO. One court appearance was dumbfounding: the judge recommended that the stalker could call her home whenever he wanted, for his daughter's sake, PPO or no PPO. Furthermore, the judge said Mary was using the PPO as a control mechanism to keep Joe away from his child and she wouldn't allow her to do that. She said he can do anything he wants when it concerns his child and if

Mary didn't let him call the house whenever he wanted to and have contact with his daughter, she would put Mary in jail!

The judge had stated that it was ridiculous that Mary and Joe, after being divorced for so long, couldn't get along. The judge stated that she can't stand PPO's and that she's bothered by them. She said that ex-spouses are using PPO's against each other to control the children and effect each other's lives in a negative way.

The judge asked "Has he physically assaulted you in the last year"? Mary answered, "No". Then the judge demanded to know why Mary needed a PPO in the first place. Mary couldn't believe it. He physically assaulted her for 6 years, while they were married and he assaulted her after they were married. He assaulted her husband, their friend's and family members. He had threatened to kill her and had held her at gunpoint. He'd been diagnosed by a psychiatrist as manic-depressive, bi-polar and alcoholic. The psychiatrist put in his file, misgivings about treating Joe as an "out patient". Mary couldn't believe, that because he hadn't assaulted her in a year, that the judge thought that she didn't need a PPO-even though the risk was still there.

Mary had a confidentiality order that asserted that she didn't have to disclose her or her husband's employment information or social security numbers for safety reasons. During court proceedings her attorney asked her what she did for a living. She said that she was a supervisor of a children's program in a domestic violence agency. The judge asked what domestic violence agency. Mary explained that she had a confidentiality order and for safety reasons didn't want to disclose that information. The judge said "Do you know what contempt is"? Mary thought, "Do I have to tell her, or go to jail"?

Discretion being the better part of valor, she told the judge where she worked. She didn't want to go to jail. The question is, is she safe from Joe-he knows where she works. She told her employer what happened. Mary was lucky in the respect that her employer was very supportive of her. She is working in a position where she is able to help other women in bad situations. Part of her strength comes from helping these women.

Mary's very conscious and aware in case he follows her to work. She is constantly aware of safety at work because of her clients and their partners. She is aware all the time to what is going on around her. She doesn't go out alone at night. When she's driving she always looks in the rearview mirror, expecting to see him at any time. It appears that when he has a love interest, she doesn't hear from him for a while. Then it starts up again, right where it left off.

The stalking has taken its toll on Mary and her family. She says that there are times that she is angry and has the strength to keep fighting this no win situation. Other times she puts her head down and cries and feels that it takes too much effort to get out of bed in the morning. Always in her mind is the question, "Will I ever have a normal life?" What keeps her going is her daughter and husband. She wants them to live a normal and happy life.

In a lot of cases children and families give impetus for stalking victims to keep going and ultimately lead successful lives.

Chapter Two

THE STALKING VICTIM

Anyone can be a victim of stalking. It doesn't matter if you're male, female (though most of the victims are, statistically, women), rich or poor. There is no one particular type of victim, and there is no particular location where a victim is stalked.

In the beginning, the situation can seem harmless. The victim may not realize that a problem is festering. The stalker may call, send flowers, cards or love letters to the victim. At this point, the victim may or may not be interested. If a victim is interested, she/he may want to pursue the relationship, until they decide that the person is not for them. If the victim is not interested, they may politely try to express their disinterest to the stalker, not wanting to hurt the stalker's feelings. Some people try to be "nice" and sympathetic towards others. These are wonderful traits, however in a stalking situation they will only make matters worse. The victim may not be dealing with a reasonable person. Trouble begins when the victim tries to shy away from the attention or tries to persuade the stalker to desist.

From the outset, the victim should be aware that stalking is abnormal, that it is not mistaken flattery and that it must be stopped quickly. If this protest is not done at once, then truly one becomes "the stalked". It is not a game, no matter how kind, sweet, or beguiling the flatterer has been before the stalking starts.

Every victim must become conscious of the hints of pending disaster: provocative phone calls, love letters of destined lives together and physical maneuvers. Whenever these designs begin, stalking, despite anyone's scorn of the issue has begun.

There is one circumstance that stands out: the victim knows the instant the "friend" has become the predator. They may try to deny it or push it aside, but the victim knows the time when the situation changes. It could be something obvious like a threatening call or it could be something more subtle, like a love letter indicating that they will be together forever. Whatever the situation is, many people don't want to believe that there is a problem, so most stalking victims don't take precautionary steps early enough to avoid the stalking situation. If they start to take precautionary steps, they are admitting that they have a problem and many don't want to believe there is a problem.

When a stalking situation starts to develop, victims may feel apprehensive, but hope that the situation will work itself out. It never does! Victims often fall into the trap of if they ignore "it", "it" will go away. Like all of us caught up in everyday life - going to work, going to school, taking the kids to school, among other responsibilities- stalking victims just don't want to deal with anything else. Their focus is on everything else but the problem that is developing. When the victim does become aware of the problem and tells family and friends of the situation, they don't want to believe anything bad is happening either. If something bad were happening they would have to deal with it. The implications of which are just too frightening.

With the media filled with horror stories of rape and murder, people's desires to be insulated from such terror is understandable. We want to think of these terrible acts as happening to someone else in another city or state. How many times have we watched the news and heard people say "I can't believe anything like that could happen *here*"? or

"Things like this just *don't* happen here." But things do happen. We may not want to accept it - but it is reality.

Society doesn't really understand what stalking victims go through. Initially, a stalking incident may seem trivial. It may even wane somewhat, but in many cases, will return to frighten the victim whenever and wherever the stalker pleases.

Stalking victims go through a range of emotions while being stalked; from flattering attention, annoyance, disbelief, anger, fear and rage. The stalking affects the victim and also the victim's family; as we've seen in Mary's case. Victims may fear for their lives and the lives of those they love. It's not unusual for the victim to ignore the stalker and to get the victim's attention, the stalker may threaten to hurt the victim's family. In some states, if immediate family members are threatened, those threats can be used as evidence.

Because of these concerns, victims' eating habits may change. They may not sleep well at night. They may have nightmares and /or may fear being attacked in their own homes. They may feel depressed because of the situation and may not know where to go for help. They may feel so overwrought and tired that their immune system is affected and they get sick. The uncertainty of stalking and its attack foist onto the victim a form of "battle fatigue". The victim doesn't know when an attack will occur or they always have to be on their guard and can never relax.

As time goes on, the stalker may pursue their victim more vigorously, with the paraphernalia mentioned earlier; cards, letters and gifts. The victim may tell the stalker of their disinterest, but the stalking continues. Family and friends may see this attention as something positive. Typical reactions include "You should feel lucky this person loves you so much" or "Why would you stop seeing someone who so obviously cares about you?" In one case, the stalker left small stuffed animals at the victim's parents' home. The victim's parents thought that it was "so nice". The police or family may not agree that there is a problem, but the victim *knows.*

After repeatedly trying to convince family and friends that they are in trouble, without success, the victim starts to reflect upon her own actions. In such a nightmarish haze of fear, uncertainty and incredulity, the victim may see herself as the cause for such a crime! It is not uncommon for victims of crime, in general, to blame themselves. This is the same with stalking victims. They try to understand what they did to cause this. (Of course they didn't do anything to cause this situation). They try to figure out what behaviors of theirs caused their stalker to relentlessly pursue them. Unfortunately, many victims believe it was their fault that they are in this situation. The result of which is that they don't get the needed help because they think that other people also think that the situation was their fault.

As the stalking increases (some slowly, some quickly) and the flattering attention turns to threats of violence, family and friends ignorantly criticize the victim. They want to know what the victim did to provoke this person. They may react by saying "If you just hadn't gone out with him" or "Why don't you just tell her your not interested, instead of playing games?" These inane questions attempt to hide or blur the predicament, which may turn easily into a crime of extreme hostility. Keep in mind that these questions come from fear and discomfort when the reality of the problem hits home.

Between the victims blaming themselves, and family and friends blaming the victim, the victim begins to feel isolated. Victims start to question their own sanity and may feel that madness is just around the corner. Often victims may feel that they are in a maze of disbelief, anxiety and helplessness. It can even get to the point where family/friends don't want to hear about the situation anymore. This imposed isolation is the drive of the stalker, whose heinous personality is fed on such desolation. He doesn't want the victim to tell anyone or do anything to disrupt his advances towards her.

Victims feel isolated from family/friends, but also isolate themselves. If they don't answer the phone or don't go out, the stalker won't call or follow them- so the stalking doesn't exist. Of course we know that the stalker does not go away. Victims may feel paralyzed from disbelieving allies and/or the loss of will.

Victims also try to isolate themselves to control their environment. They may close their world down to gain control over their lives. They try to escape psychologically, and who wouldn't in these shuddering circumstances? The strain of dealing with the situation is often more than some victims can tolerate.

In one case, a 25-year-old man, Tony, was stalked by a 23-year-old female, who he dated for 2 months. After breaking off the relationship with her, she began stalking him for over 6 years. During various stages of the stalking, he would not leave his home, unless it was absolutely necessary, in the hope that the situation didn't really exist. But of course it did.

Tony wondered how it had gotten to that point of not wanting to leave his home. It began innocently enough. He met his stalker at a bar.

44

Their eyes met and she had waived to him to dance with her. He did. Later in the evening they met at a local restaurant and exchanged phone numbers. She seemed like a nice girl. There wasn't a big physical attraction on his part, but she seemed like a normal, amiable young woman from a pleasant family.

They dated for a few months, but their relationship didn't evolve into much. He decided to cut it off before it went too far. He told her he wanted to break it off. She called him 6-8 weeks after they broke up. At the time, he didn't think that this was anything out of the ordinary. She's been calling ever since.

She started with calling on a daily basis. She would show up at his work, send flowers, letters and pictures. She even went as far as to fake a pregnancy when they first broke up. Thinking that it "would all blow over", he tried to take all of this pestering in stride. He just lived with it. To make things worse, she began telephoning him in the early hours of the morning. It was frightening. He didn't tell his parents at the beginning, because he thought that it was his problem.

Almost driven crazy, (after two and a half years of torment), Tony finally called the police. He couldn't get it through to her not to show up at his work. She kept calling and showing up at his work so much that other employees were becoming concerned. He called the police because she was showing up 3-4 times a day. She left his work everytime he said he would call the police. Even though he contacted the police a number of times, the police never talked to her. They did go to his work to file a complaint but they didn't take the situation too seriously. In fact, he was asked, sarcastically, why he had let the situation go on for so long. He said he thought she would just go away.

Sometimes Tony would go out into the parking lot and talk to her because he thought if he talked to her, he could get her to leave him alone. It didn't work. They would be in the parking lot talking for half an hour. She'd ramble on and make up stuff to talk to him about. She analyzed everything that he said. She didn't want to let him go. She said that they would be together forever.

Eventually, Tony had set up a phone tap and recorded her messages. As time went on, he wouldn't hear from her for 2-3 months so he erased all of her messages. He thought it was over. Then she would start again. One time he was at a bar with his friends, and was talking to a female friend. She came in, spit in his face and ran out.

During this time, whenever he would try to talk to her about her behavior, she didn't respond to his questions. She would talk about her stress and worries and that she didn't need to be alone "right now." When she called his girlfriend and threatened his mother, he couldn't believe what was happening. It pushed him over the edge.

Tony went to circuit court to file a PPO. She in turn filed a PPO against him, with no documentation! It was her word against his. This is a common occurrence in many stalking cases. "The problem with this is that the Legislature has said that you are to proceed on the word of the person who comes to court," said Judge Edward Sosnick of Oakland County Family Court.[15]

Well, they went to court. The judge didn't see the seriousness of the case. Since there was no physical contact only calls and letters, he said to both of them to leave each other alone. When asked what he would like to happen to resolve this case, Tony said he would like her to go to jail. He wants peace again in his life.

During this ordeal he kept asking himself "Do I deserve this?" In retrospect, he thinks she stalked him because she was trying hard to get married and have kids. She always talked about that. He wasn't ready for that and told her. Also, he has a good family, a good job and a promising career and those were things she wanted.

Tony thought his stalker believed she could change what he thought about her. She thought he'd come around. He said he never hurt her and doesn't want to have to go around looking over his shoulder. He's gotten through this with the help of his family and friends along with his inner strength. He is now going on with his life.

Tony's advice to stalking victims is to go to the police at the beginning and document everything. He says, "Don't wait because it will never end. Go to the police before someone gets killed."

In Tony's case, the stalker tried to look like the victim, and it basically worked. It is not uncommon for the stalker to portray himself/herself as the victim. In one case, Diane, was having an on-again off-again relationship with her boyfriend. The boyfriend was seeing someone else at the same time he was seeing Diane. During this time, Diane kept receiving hang-ups. She thought they were from the 'other' woman. Evidently, every time the boyfriend appeared to be going back with Diane, something would happen. Diane's neighbors would tell her that a woman would come around asking questions about her. Her neighbors were very sharp and didn't tell the woman anything. Diane was lucky in the respect that in many cases, stalkers find out information by asking neighbors questions and appearing likeable and innocent.

Sometimes when she left work in the evening, someone would try to follow her home. It even got to the point that once, when Diane and the boyfriend were away on vacation, the 'other' woman came and banged on their hotel room door! In a desperate attempt to keep the boyfriend, the other woman kept telling him *she* was the one being stalked and harassed.

One night when Diane came home from work, she noticed she had received a phone call. She hit *69 (a feature that rang the last number called) and her boyfriend answered. The boyfriend was at the 'other' woman's house. She could hear the other woman screeching in the background saying, "See *she's* harassing and stalking *me!*" The other woman filed a PPO against Diane!

Diane was angry and aggravated. She knew she didn't do anything wrong - yet it looked like she did. She went to the police station and explained her story. The sergeant on duty advised her to also file a PPO. He said that the 'other' woman could accuse Diane of something and they would have to act on it. She asked him what about all the calls she had documented. Every time the woman called, Diane's *caller ID*, registered the words 'private number.' He said that those calls were not proof, because anyone could have made the calls. In Diane's case, she was being stalked by the 'other' woman, but the 'other' woman turned the situation to her advantage.

In a different situation, where the victim was accused of being a stalker, but wasn't one, involved a college student named Don. He had dated a girl for a few months but then she wanted to break up. Don said he called her a couple of times to find out what the problem was and what went wrong. For his trouble, he got a PPO filed against him.

He was shocked! He couldn't believe that he was being accused of stalking her! They had to go to court. He wanted to fight the accusation but his parents were concerned that if he lost, he may have to spend some time in jail. He didn't want to take the plea bargain that was offered, but his parents said they thought that it was the best way to go. So he plead guilty and received one year probation and had to do some community service. He wasn't happy with the whole situation but just wanted to put the whole thing behind him.

A different variation of when someone says they're being stalked, but they're not, is called, False Victimization. It is where an individual, usually female, needs to be the center of attention. They believe that their relationship is dissolving and aspire to revitalize it.

The following is a *verbatim* example from J. Reid Meloy's book, *The Psychology of Stalking*.

"For example, a woman believed that her husband was having an affair with his secretary. She fabricated a police report, stating that a man forced his way into her home and attacked her with a knife, causing numerous lacerations. She provided a very detailed description of the perpetrator. As expected, this caused a good deal of alarm for her husband. This event was followed up by a series of threatening notes left on her front porch.

One night when her husband was away she claimed to see the suspect in her back yard. She fired several rounds at him with her handgun. Again, a police report was completed and the local police division continued to expend resources to apprehend the suspect. All these events caused her husband to begin to take his wife to work with him to ensure her safety. Ultimately, the TMU assumed the case and a video camera caught the woman depositing one of the threatening letters on her own doorstep. When confronted, she admitted to fabricating the entire story in order to refocus her husband's attention onto herself." [16]

Unfortunately, these cases take time and effort to investigate and take away valuable time from people who need it. It may also give police negative ideas about the crime of stalking. When they encounter a situation like this, it gives us a broader perspective as to why they may question a victim's story.

STALKING CASE: THREE

"He pointed the gun at her head and said he would blow her head off"

Susan had 3 small boys. Her husband had been killed in a car accident. She was an independent working mother. Then she met David. They met through a mutual friend. He was rude and obnoxious when they first met. She wasn't sure she even liked him but he was very persistent in his quest for her. He would ask, "Can I come over"? When Susan said, "No. I'm going out" he would still come over before she left. Once he arrived, it was hard to get him to leave.

As time went on, they wrongfully decided that they should give up their dwellings and live together to save rent. Susan wasn't sure if he was the one for her, but at this point in her life she was vulnerable. She needed extra support and a support system.

The economic savings in rent did not prepare her for David's assault the first night they had moved in together. He resented her having gone out with a girlfriend for coffee, so he beat her.

Susan eventually left him because of the physical assaults. She had not been brought up in that type of environment. She had never had that happen to her before. By mistaking economics for a reason, she fell victim to a tyrant. She was embarrassed by her decision to be with him, which caused so much needless suffering, including hospitalization for plastic surgery on her face. She was afraid of his threats about 'knocking her teeth out'. He would cut up her clothes when he got mad. He did this so she couldn't go anywhere. She had

51

to keep buying new clothes and that got pretty expensive over tim.

David didn't have to have a reason to assault her. He assaulted her when he thought she was talking back to him or if she came home late. David's behavior was not always predictable. Sometimes he would walk in and knock Susan off her chair. Other times she could tell how he would be by how he closed the car door. He always tried to control her. He'd take the telephone out of the house so she couldn't make calls. He'd take the keys to the car so she couldn't go out. In those cases she took the bus. He'd leave bruises so she was too embarrassed to go to school or work.

David was fanatical about cleanliness. He wanted the house to be spotless. Susan had to wipe the water spots from the tub whenever someone took a shower. The house had to be hospital clean. Basking in his control, David was very strict on what time the kids went to bed and what time they got up. He thought that children "should be seen and not heard".

It got to the point, that if there were crumbs on the kitchen table, David would beat her severely. Embarrassed, Susan hid this situation from her family and friends.

She did not call the police right away because he said he'd kill her. She thought that if she did call the police, she would be physically assaulted even worse. Finally, she did call the police because he had sexually assaulted her. The police couldn't do anything. They said there was no law against a married woman being sexually assaulted by her husband. She didn't feel that there was any help for her.

The last straw for her came when David returned from California and assaulted her because she didn't pick him up from the airport. When she got home he grabbed her by the coat collar and started shaking her. She got away from him. He said he'd "Ice her ass". He said he was willing to spend time in jail and that no one would care if she were dead. Her blood ran cold. Four days later Susan left him.

After she separated from David, the stalking started. He had tried to break into her home more than once. One night when she saw that someone had tried to get into her home, Susan called the police. The police said someone had gone up to all the windows and attempted to get in. Luckily, she had special locks on the windows and doors that prevented him from doing so. Eventually, she had moved out of state. She had not told anyone where she was. After three weeks of being "hidden" she came home and David was sitting on the couch!

When he wanted to find her, he'd drive through neighborhoods and look at rows and rows of mailboxes to see if he could see her name. He had a friend in the Secretary of State's office who would provide him with information that he wanted. Once, acting like a concerned husband, he even filed a missing persons report on her at the police station. She called the police department and explained her situation. They told her to keep doing what she was doing.

Another time, he shot at her house. It was her birthday. She wasn't feeling well so she went to her room to rest. She happened to look out the bedroom window. There was David, revealed by the streetlight, crouching by the car. He walked towards her home, shooting a gun. She ran into the living room and told her family to get down. They called the police. The state and local police responded very quickly.

Another incident occurred one morning when Susan took the trash out. When she went back out approximately forty-five minutes later, she had a flat tire. The tire had been slashed. Another time, she drove to the store. When she came out, the car wouldn't start. It finally started. She found out that the battery had been cut just enough that it didn't make a good connection.

Overtime the stalking escalated to kidnapping.

One morning at about 7:30 am, Susan parked her car and was proceeding to go into work. It was a big parking lot, far from the street. All of a sudden someone came up behind her. It was David. He grabbed her arm. She told him to let her go. He said "No you're coming with me." He had a gun. He forced her to get into the car. He held on to her arm as he made her crawl across the front seat. He drove them downtown to a friend's house. There he held her hostage and wouldn't let her leave his sight. He pointed the gun at her head and said that he'd blow her head off. Then he sexually assaulted her.

At one point when she went to use the bathroom, she was able to sneak the phone in and call for help. Because of her call, her family knew where she was and called the police. The police called the house. David said if the phone rang again, he'd strangle her and leave her in the bed. He always had the gun. She thought he was going to kill her and then himself. The SWAT team broke into the house and saved her. He had kept her hostage for almost twenty-four hours.

David spent four and one half years in prison for the kidnapping. When he was getting out, Susan bought a handgun and obtained a concealed weapons permit. She knew that at this point that it would be him or her. She didn't want it to be her. As with many victims, the time comes when they will tolerate abuse no longer, despite the cost.

She did not plan to be abused anymore! Two and a half weeks after he was let out of prison, she was sitting on her porch. She saw him driving up and down her street.

Susan learned that the courts look at documentation. If a victim can prove a history of the stalker's behavior, it will help their case. Susan obtained a personal protection order when she divorced David. It did not keep him away from her. He still tried to find her. However, it helped with the paper trail and with law enforcement. The police came quicker when she said she had a personal protection order.

Before the stalking law, the police did what they could to help Susan. They would come out and make sure he was no longer on the property. After the stalking law went into effect, the police were able to be more effective in dealing with David. Susan is very glad that a person can now be convicted of stalking. However, she feels that the penalty for a second offense should be harsher.

The police have been very supportive and helpful. Susan has a wonderful working relationship with the police. Everytime David comes back into the city, the detective calls and notifies her.
The sheriffs department and local police detectives have set up a plan if he turns up. David is a convicted stalker and faces severe punishment should he attempt criminal behavior again.

Susan is currently married to another man and her children are grown. In retrospect, she didn't think David ever loved her. He wanted someone to control. He had said he loved her but his actions and words showed that this was not always the truth.

After interviewing Susan, I was surprised that a woman as strong as

she was, could ever experience what she went through. I didn't understand it-how could that happen? During my research I found that domestic violence can happen to *anyone*. "Women who are physically strong, emotionally together, financially successful, socially accepted, and even spiritually ahead of most other women fall into the trap of domestic violence just as less healthy women do".
17

Susan was at a time in her life where she was vulnerable, made a bad decision and suffered because of it, for years. She was independent, intelligent and a hardworking woman and mother. She could always support herself and her children. This strength is what got her through all these years and is continuing to help her now, though the road has been a hard one. However, to this day she still has anxiety. She doesn't know where David is.

She is hyper-vigilant. She doesn't go out by herself. She doesn't know when he'll show up and she has to be ready for when he does. She has both physical and emotional scars, but today she is very happy. She is currently working at a safe house, helping women who are in similar situations. She has testified to the House and Senate Judicial Committee in favor of the stalking law.

Chapter Three

Domestic Violence Stalking

The majority of stalking cases result from relationships that have crumbled. Many of us enter into relationships expecting that the relationship will work-that we will have a happy relationship and that our dreams will come true. In Susan's case, initially, she wasn't sure if he was the one, but she thought she was in love with him. Susan mistook necessity for love, and a man's persistence for respect. A mistake in affection nearly cost her life! She mirrors so many victims even today. Over time when she separated from David, she worked two jobs and was going to school. Here again she shows strength and independence. She said she lived a quiet peaceful and happy life. She didn't want to live a life of being controlled and assaulted.

Susan had had enough. She refused to live under this demanding and controlling man any longer. In general, when a stalking victim tries to end the relationship the stalker uses intimidation to regain control over the victim. As we've seen with Susan when David threatened her. Dr. Gary Kaufmann, Chief Psychologist, Michigan State Police Behavioral Science Section, explains what may happen in domestic stalking situations. "It happens when a woman says, I've had enough of this relationship and I don't want to be involved with you. Often times, when the stalker is expelled from the relationship, that's when we see the stalking begin. It is motivated by a variety of emotions. It is a combination of anger and resentment for being expelled. Out of vengeance they harass the victim. They want to control the victim's life. They send the message, you can break up but I'll always be there as an intimidator. I will always be out there someplace and influence your world". [18]

To this day, 10-12 years after the kidnapping, David is still influencing Susan's world. She says she never feels 100% safe but she feels as safe as she can. She would only feel 100% safe if David were dead. Susan was speaking sincerely and from the heart. She was simply stating a fact.

When I asked Susan what she would like other women to know who are in similar situations, she said that if anyone is in an abusive relationship to "Get Out". Go to a shelter and develop a safety plan. She says to leave and don't go back.

Susan survived because of the support she received from a lot of people. She said blame should not go on the victim. She says that the blame is on the batterer because they caused the situation to happen. She believes that the survivors are innocent because before they know what is going on they are already pulled into the situation and it's hard to get out. She felt that leaving is not an option for all women because their partners or husbands prevent that from happening.

Dr. Gary Kaufmann, expands upon his ideas pertaining to stalking and domestic situations. He theorized that many stalkers have a stereotypical view of women. Thinking that all females are dependant, nurturing and caring, stalkers, may angrily act if that sense of 'maternalism' is challenged. Many stalkers believe women will carry out their maternal role. "From a psychological level, the underlying issue for a lot of stalking behavior in domestic situations is almost a mother/child relationship where the child is acting out because of attempted abandonment and is attempting to continue to maintain the relationship"[19]

In Susan's case, there was a previous relationship with her stalker and the potential for her situation to have ended violently. The National Victim Center, has categorized stalking situations where a previous relationship existed between the victim and stalker as "Simple Obsession" stalkings. These situations make up about 70-80% of stalking cases. These are also known as "fatal attraction" cases. "The most likely group of stalkers to be violent are the simple obsessionals, those individuals who have had a prior sexually intimate relationship with the victim" [20]

Simple Obsession stalking cases fall into the realm of personality disorder cases. These stalkers: 1) generally are socially incompetent and have very low self-esteem; 2) the stalker's self-esteem is linked to the relationship with the victim. They see themselves as an extension to the victim. If they lose the victim, they lose their self-esteem. If the stalker looses their self-esteem, in their mind, they are nothing. They will go to any length to keep the victim. They may also see the person as a possession.

When the woman leaves or attempts to leave, the man cannot accept the rejection and does not want to let the woman leave. The man then will threaten, harass or assault the woman to make her stay. This behavior has been referred to as "separation assault" by experts. In some domestic violence stalking situations, after the woman attempts to leave the relationship, the stalking will begin.

Studies have been done to determine reasons why women stay in abusive relationships. Lenore E. Walker, one of the leading authorities in the area of spousal abuse presented the concept of the "Battered Woman Syndrome". "According to Walker, the battered woman syndrome theorizes that victims of spousal abuse gradually become immobilized by fear and believe they have no other options."[21]

Susan was successfully able to break free from her domestic violence situation and she is doing all she can about the stalking situation. It wasn't easy for her. But she is a survivor.

There is not a lot of data on stalking and its relationship to domestic violence. However, there does appear to be a relationship between stalking and controlling behavior.

" A clear relationship existed between stalking and other emotionally controlling and physically abusive behavior. About half of the female stalking victims had been stalked by a current or former marital or cohabiting partner. About 80 percent of these women were, at some point in the relationship, physically assaulted by that partner, and 31 percent were sexually assaulted." [22]

In their quest to control the victim, the predator's jealousy demands a lone confiscation of the victim, "Because of this intense jealousy, when future stalkers are dating, they will often want to spend every second possible with the individuals they've become involved with, and will try to keep the individuals from having any contact at all with anyone of the opposite sex". [23]

Domestic violence stalkers want to dominate their victims. In their mind they "have the right and responsibility to keep the person in line" and the right and responsibility to enforce it. They truly believe that the "victim belongs to them and is theirs to control." If the victim somehow does escape or leave the stalker, he feels it's his right to punish her for escaping. This is when the stalker conveys to the victim "If I can't have you no one else will." They are deadly serious.

Anyone or anything that the victim is interested in threatens the stalker's 'sense of supremacy', which in turn may foster homicidal and/or suicidal tendencies. This was particularly demonstrated in Carol's case. Many of the stalkers that I have interviewed, fell under the domestic violence category. Many of them did not identify themselves as predators or as criminals. Also, many of them had no clue of the stalking law. The first they learned of it was when they went to court. One stalker said he went to the library and looked up what stalking was after being charged with it!

The impact of domestic violence is coming more and more into the spotlight. Some researchers believe that in up to 80% of stalking cases there is some form of domestic connection.
"Directors of domestic violence shelters and coalitions across the country confirm the link between stalking behavior and domestic abuse." [24]

In helping to explain the dynamics of family violence and to better understand why victims remain in abusive relationships, Lenore E. Walker developed the concept of the "cycle theory of violence".
    Her theory has three phases. They are:
        1. tension building phase,
        2. the explosion or acute battering phase,
        3. the calm, loving respite phase.
These phases may or may not all occur exactly the same for everyone. It depends on the relationship. It is my understanding, that one reason why victims remain in abusive relationships is because once the third

phase begins, there is the hope that the abuse will end. Similar to stalking cases, usually the intolerable situation doesn't just end.

In domestic stalking cases there is a similar cycle. The following are three hypothetical phases in the cycle of stalking by Wendy Collier of the Colorado based Victim Protection Services.

The first phase is the "Tensions Building Phase". This is where there are phone calls, gifts, threats. In this phase the stalker attempts to control the victim.

The second phase is the "Explosive or Acutely Violent Phase". This involves kidnapping, rape, violence against the victims family and friends, murder and suicide.

The third phase is the "Hearts and Flowers Phase". The person says that they are sorry. There may be periods of silence. The victim thinks the stalking is over. They may let their guard down which may put them at risk of attack. Eventually the stalking may resume.

In Mary's case, the stalking would stop whenever the ex-husband had a new love interest. When that ended, the stalking would resume. Every situation is unique and not everyone experiences these phases.

On a positive note it should be said that not all women stay. "Up to 75 percent of those reporting abuse have left, permanently. But leaving has not exactly been the end of their problems: many have been followed, even stalked, harassed, and assaulted by former husbands or boyfriends. Many others have left only to return. The point, though, is that women don't just sit there and take it forever."[25]

STALKING CASE: FOUR

"He knocked her down and started choking her..."

Joan met her stalker at college while she was doing research; he worked there. Dating for one month, Joan found out that he was a science student who worked as a security officer. Joan was attracted to 'Bill' because of his quick intelligence, looks and breeding. Bill was quiet and this intrigued Joan, even when he would stumble over answers about his past. Joan suspected that the reticence was part of his personality, but, later, she saw this as a warning sign of trouble ahead.

The relationship developed to some extent but they didn't go out a lot. During their short relationship there were other warning signs. Though her friends seemed uneasy and uncomplimentary about Bill, Joan wanted to draw her own conclusions, though she appreciated the 'friendly concern'. However, there was something about Bill that bothered her, but she didn't know exactly what it was. The time came for the dating to end. Three weeks of trying to end the relationship came and went. She tried to let him down easy (she is not one to hurt people) and asserting, politely her own independence, Joan finally was forced to demand the dating stop! This was the cue for the predator to stalk the quarry.

"An axiom of the stalking dynamic: Men who cannot let go choose women who cannot say no. Most victims will concede that even thought they wanted to they were initially reluctant to explicitly reject. Often, the niceness or delicacy of a woman's rejection is taken as affection".[26]

Joan is a decent and caring person. She didn't want to hurt Bill. She was more concerned about his feelings than she was about herself. She pitied his hurt ego, more than she protected her own. Like Joan, many women fall into this trap: "If the culture taught and then allowed women to explicitly reject and to say no, or if more women took that power early in every relationship, stalking cases would decline dramatically."[27]

Before the stalking, it seemed that he understood that they were going to be friends and would back off. Then he would show up all the time. He would show up at her work and sit there for hours (annoying her by his presence). Though Joan joked about this with friends, she was beginning to worry that the predicament was "rather creepy". She remembered the night she wanted to break up with him. Her decision to end the relationship took five hours, in a parking lot, to explain to Bill that they could be friends and nothing more. She kept trying to explain that he didn't do any thing wrong. She told him that she just didn't think that he was the one for her.

Trying to find some way so that Bill would leave her alone, Joan confided to Bill that she still loved her ex-boyfriend. Bill became incensed. Even if the victim says that she has a significant other, the stalker still thinks he has a chance. "When a woman explains why she is rejecting, this type of man will challenge each reason she offers. I suggest that women never explain why they don't want a relationship but simply make clear that they have thought it over, that this is their decision, and that they expect the man to respect it" [28]

One night she went out to her car after work and saw something under the wiper on the driver's side. It was a note. At that point, notes were left on her car with profanities written on them. She was followed and harassed. She realized that she was being stalked after the 3rd incident when she was driving along and noticed he was behind her! He would show up out of the blue. She would be driving around her hometown and suddenly he'd be there. When she went to the police, the initial reaction was: "Do you still want to date this person?" She thought that was ridiculous. If she still wanted to date this individual she would be working the situation out instead of informing the police that he's stalking her!

The police went to Bill's home and in a fatherly way told him to stop his behavior or else. He didn't listen to them. Joan was angry and troubled because she had never had a situation like this before and never been involved with anyone who was like this. It made her think twice about doing things such as walking out to her car. She said she felt trapped and she couldn't enjoy herself without worrying that *he* would be popping up out of nowhere.

When Joan got upset she would go through a phase when she would talk to a friend about the problem. The friend would say that Joan had the right to be where she wanted to be. That Joan had as much right as the stalker had. Then Joan would get angry and do what she wanted to do. However, always in the back of Joan's mind was the concern that "it wasn't a matter of if, but a matter of when he was going to pop up again". To this day when she drives she is always looking in the rear view mirror.

The police were finally able to intervene formally, when he assaulted her-approximately two years after the stalking began. Joan was told by the municipality where she lived that she needed to present Bill with a letter stating that should he be seen at her residence that he would be charged with trespassing. She went to the college where he was, with the letter. She was accompanied by security officers, and presented the letter to him. Then she and the security officers left the building. He shoved his way right past the security officers, knocked her down and started choking her!

She thought that the security officers were surprised because nothing really happened at the college except parking tickets or accidents.

Two years prior to the assault, the police didn't help her because Bill had committed no crime. They did the best they could based on the limitations of the law. They could see she had a problem, but as long as the stalker stayed within the law, there was nothing they could do. They also advised her to document any contact with him. She went through a 2-year scenario of "documenting, documenting, documenting". She saw him everywhere she went. Each time she was told to write it down and she did.

She kept a journal of what happened to her. The police said documentation was important, but she didn't understand why because they never did anything with it until he assaulted her. She documented when he came by her house, work and school. She wrote down when he followed her. She kept all the letters and pictures. She said it was a sickening feeling. She wanted to burn or throw away the things he gave her, but she was forced to keep them. It made her sick to keep everything. However, she had to keep it all until she could use it in court so that the stalking would stop. The police also told her that she could file a restraining order against him. If he violated it, then he could go to court. She didn't have the time or the money to do this because she was in graduate school.

In 1990 Bill was charged with simple assault and battery. He received two years of probation. The attack was frightening but she finally had something on him. He violated the probation within a week of the assault. The same pattern of pursuit, gifts, notes and cards followed. He followed Joan to work and left notes on her car. He went near her residence again. The police advised her that she had to prove he was there. They told her to take a picture of Bill lurking around the property. The police had to have evidence of his whereabouts. They would look at the picture and based upon houses in the neighborhood, they could tell whether he was there or not. She couldn't believe she had to do this. She was the one complaining and needed the help. He was invading her life and he was getting away with it. She was angry because he enjoyed his life. He could go anywhere he wanted to and do whatever he wanted to, but she couldn't.

Bill sent her many letters. Some started out with "Dear" and ended with "Love". He wrote of how much he loved her, to what a "harlot" she was. The letters were as ungrammatical as they were absurd. Over 8 years she had been stalked. He became progressively more angry and violent. The letters went from "I love you" to "I hate you".

There would be a lot of contact, then it would peak. Then he would just disappear. His contact would run in cycles. Because of his disappearance the police would say that he went away. They would ask her what she was worried about because she hadn't heard from him in two months. She knew he would show up again-it was his pattern.

In 1993 when the stalking law was in effect, Bill left a package at Joan's parents home. Joan went to the police. They were frustrated at not being able to help. She filed a PPO because she wanted to be left alone. Bill was ruling her actions and restraining her from living. She felt she had to do *something*.

She thinks that in his own way Bill loved her. She thought that there were many reasons why he stalked her. She thought that Bill's stalking resulted from his insecurity, unrequited love, poor upbringing and purposeless in life. According to her, his purpose in life was to find out what she was doing and make her pay for the pain she caused him. She didn't know what he exactly wanted from her. She thought he wanted to play mind games and he wanted to have control over her.

Looking back, Joan felt that in some respect she deserved his anger because she broke up with him. She may have had some guilty feelings that she was hurting him. She thought that if he vented his anger and frustration, he'd get it out of his system. He didn't.

She thinks that stalkers in general, need to feel in control. They need to know they push that persons "buttons". She knows that stalkers instill fear and anger. Joan said that her stalker was the "puppeteer" and that she was the "puppet". She said that when she cut the strings and confronted him, it angered him and made him lash out.

When she was dating, he got more aggravated and more things occurred. This was very frustrating because she knew that it wasn't something she did but it was the consequences of his actions. It was a constant reminder that he was out there. Besides the fear and anxiety that the stalker caused her, Joan spent a lot of time defending her name and fighting the stigma that stalking inevitably brings. She felt that her only fault was that she existed. It was hard enough going to school and work but she also had to clear her name and file reports.

One day when she went to work, her car was keyed. She had parked in the middle of the lot. No one else's car had been keyed, but at that time she didn't think it was him. At least she was hoping that it wasn't him. When it happened again, she *knew* it was Bill. The security department put a camera up in the parking garage and they caught him on tape, slashing the roof of her car!

What was particularly frightening to Joan, was Bill's determination to find out what she was doing and to find out information that involved her. The terrifying truth was that Bill knew Joan's whereabouts, knew her family history, and even investigated acquaintances of hers. He was everywhere at once, or so it seemed. At times the situation was very unnerving for her.

If she was followed she pulled into a police station and filed a report. When she went out with a male friend, Bill would follow them. One time when she and a friend were followed, they pulled into a police station. Bill left. Two days later the police called her. Bill had accused her friend of running him off the road!

Joan cautions against "falling for the handsome type," because her stalker looked like he just stepped out of GQ magazine. She says that you can't identity a stalker by his looks. She recommends that women should not go out late at night. She also recommends always have your keys in hand, walk with confidence and lock your doors. Other recommendations are to leave your gas tank filled and if you work late, close the blinds so no one can watch you without you being aware of it. She stresses not to be scared all the time, but to be careful. One learning aspect that came out of her situation, was that she learned how to be assertive and learned how to make her own feelings valuable.

Currently she is not being stalked. Bill went to jail for malicious destruction of property and stalking. He was in jail for 8 month's but the sentence was cut to three months because of good behavior. Even though he will be on a tether when he's released, she is still concerned about what he'll do. She now has a new boyfriend. When that boyfriend is out of town, she sleeps in her room with the door locked and with a gun. She is constantly looking over her shoulder. She now looks underneath the car, in the back seat, and is cognizant of her surroundings. She told me that women should be doing this any way, but unfortunately it takes something to happen before we do take precautions.

Today, Joan wants nothing to do with Bill. She just wants to go on with her life. Presently she feels good but does not know when Bill will reappear-to begin the nightmare anew. She is more assertive with relationships. If a co-worker asks her out and is persistent, the hairs go up on the back of her neck. She is still affected and she says she drives with her eyes forward and backward. She has learned from her experience. She learned that there are no guarantees in life and a person doesn't have to hold on to guilt feelings that they might have hurt someone. That a person has rights to freedom and no one has the right to take it away from you.

Joan's stalking has changed her life forever, but she tries to be positive. She concentrates on the good issues in life and how every experience involves learning. When she feels bad, she thinks about what she went through and how things would have been if she never met Bill. The stalking has opened her eyes on how people really act. To be strong, means that one must face people realistically, without illusions. She is a strong person who wants to make a happy life for herself. Regardless of being stalked, she is determined to successfully go on with her life.

Chapter Four

PROFILE OF A STALKER

There are many concepts as to what type of person stalks another human being. We wish that the stalker had a certain look or identifiable mannerism. Unfortunately, that is not the case. Stalkers look like everyone else. In Joan's case, Bill looked like someone who could have posed for GQ magazine! There is no fool proof way to tell who a stalker is. Stalkers are human beings in appearance, work, and socialization. It is their mode of crime that sets such an offender apart from normality. Each stalker and stalking situation is unique unto itself.

Unfortunately, when you meet someone they don't tell you that they are a stalker. If only it could be that easy. If anything, many stalkers are very adept at fooling those around them. They come across as very charming and attentive. They are able to hide their true personality for an extended period of time. The qualities that initially drew the victim to the stalker, in most of the stalking cases that I have researched, were that the stalker appeared very attractive, charming and attentive. They came across so well, that the victims initially saw their future tormentors as wondrous.

Another quality that stood out, was that they were on the quiet side. At first, this was considered a good quality. Later it was discovered that the stalker had a potentially violent temperament. Again, there is no universal stalker profile: stalkers have as many varied characteristics as any other person in the world.

73

Many women have an idea in their mind of the type of person they want to have a relationship with. In their mind, they know who the perfect person is for them. The stalker plays upon the fantasy of what kind of man, relationship and life the woman yearns for. When the victim meets the stalker, not only does this person seem perfect, but almost exceeds what the victim is looking for. This attraction, peppered with a little control, can be seductively charming.

Stalkers can be men or women. It's a gender-neutral crime. However, current research indicates there are more male stalkers then female stalkers.

Most of stalking cases are men stalking women. This doesn't mean that women don't stalk men or men don't stalk men or women do not stalk other females. There are cases of each. The following quote gives a broader perspective as to who is stalked by whom.

" Most victims knew their stalker. Women were significantly more likely to be stalked by an intimate partner--whether that partner was a current spouse, a former spouse or cohabiting partner, or a date. Only 21 percent of stalkers identified by female victims were strangers. On the other hand, men were significantly more likely to be stalked by a stranger or an acquaintance. About 87 percent of stalkers were men. Women tended to be victimized by lone stalkers, but in 50 percent of male victimization's the stalker had an accomplice--usually a friend or girlfriend." [29]

Since stalking behavior is frightening and threatening, questions arise as to what would cause this type of behavior. There are numerous explanations concerning stalking behavior. Many stalkers suffer from

74

mental disorders. "It is estimated that 90 percent of stalkers suffer from at least one kind of mental disorder, which can include different forms of obsession and delusions". [30]

Some suffer from a delusional disorder, called erotomania. The stalker believes that their fantasies are true. *Erotomania* is also called *erotomanic delusions.* It is not new. It has been reported since ancient times.

Erotomania is interesting because it is the delusional belief that one person is passionately loved by another. Many celebrity stalkers fall into this category. In the stalker's mind, the victim loves the stalker. In reality, the celebrity usually has no knowledge of the person, until confronted.

"The delusion is frequently one of an idealized love, a "perfect match". The person is convinced that the object, usually of the opposite sex, fervently loves him or her, and would return the affection if not for some external influence. The onset of symptoms is sudden; the person often has had only brief or not prior contact with the object. They believe that actions, events, or otherwise usual behaviors by the object take on special meaning specifically intended for the person. He or she rejects any evidence to the contrary and typically remains delusional for years (3,4)." [31]

With a denial or rebuff, the stalker often escalates his predatory quest for the victim and may become violent. Along with celebrities, victims of such aberrant stalkers are commonly public figures or persons of higher economic class and status. Individuals suffering from this delusion may contact the victim despite obstacles in their path.

Though research has been done on erotomania, how to treat it effectively and what causes it, is still unclear. "Besides enforced hospitalization, there is very little effective treatment, although drug therapy and intensive psychiatry have proved of some use. No one is sure what causes erotomanica". [32]

In the book, *I Know You Really Love Me,* author, Doreen Orion, a psychiatrist was stalked by her patient. Her stalker suffered from erotomania, but the scenario was unusual, at least statistically so, for the stalker was female. One day her patient after being approached about her portion of her bill, began screaming and pulling her hair. The psychiatrist explained that as long as the patient could prove that she couldn't pay her bill, the hospital and she would accept only the insurance payment. The patient at first didn't believe her. Dr. Orion explained that the hospital and she did this routinely for patients.

Dr. Orion continued to see the patient until she was discharged. After the patient was discharged, Dr. Orion received a note from her. It read: "I was surprised, flattered, by your interest, since I know you and Dr. J. are an item. Hope we can pursue, but if don't respond, I'll understand" and included her phone number." [33]
Dr. Orion questioned whether the patient took her "routine kindness" for something other then what it was. As a result, Dr. Orion was stalked for a number of years regardless of the number of times she told her stalker to stop her pursuit.

According the National Victim Center, there are stalkers, who are called, love-obsessed stalkers. Their schizophrenia or paranoia, is focused on someone they don't have a relationship with. This group makes up about 20-25% of stalking cases. They may consist of casual acquaintances or stranger stalkings.

In one case, Nancy, an attractive and outgoing college student was being stalked by a stranger. Nancy would go to class and return to her car after class. One day, there was a single sheet of white paper with a black 'X' on the windshield of her car. This strange action persisted for about a week. Nancy suspected her friends of teasing her; however, when her automobile was ransacked, and her books stolen, she knew trouble was hers! The books, marred with an X, were returned one by one on her porch.

Nancy knew that she had little evidence, so she did not consult the police, which she should have done. A victim should never wait for more torment in stalking predicaments. The next incident pushed her into action.

One afternoon, she received a knock on the door and was greeted by a Valentine's gift of boxed roses. When she opened the box she found 12 dead black roses. It was addressed - "from an admirer." Nancy went to the police who contacted the florist immediately. The florist described the buyer: a male in his 20's with blond hair, who paid in cash. The florist told the police that the flowers he sold had not been dead. Also, the florist had never seen the customer before. That's where the lead ended.

The next harassment saw Nancy's gym locker broken into by the "unknown" stalker. She notified the establishment who coincidentally had a security camera directed at the door of the locker room. The police were notified. They were able to develop a black/white picture of a white male leaving the female locker room. However, the photograph was dark and grainy, so stark identification proved impossible.

From what she could make out, Nancy had never seen this individual before. The police investigated but couldn't come up with much information. After that, some time went by without incident.

Then one day while Nancy was studying, she let her small dog out in the backyard. She lived in a home where the backyard was enclosed with a privacy fence. About 20 minutes later, she called her dog back in. Attached to the dogs collar was a black ribbon. It was a message to her. The stalker had access to her at anytime. The "phantom" continues to stalk her. To this day, she doesn't know who is stalking her. She continues to go to school and work.

Another example of a stranger stalking happened to Bonnie Campbell the Director of Violence Against Women Office, the U.S. Department of Justice. She was stalked several years ago. She served as State Chair of the Iowa Democratic Party from 1987 to 1989. During this time the Presidential caucuses were occurring in Iowa. There was a lot of political activity in Iowa, and as a result of this she received a considerable amount of media exposure. It was during this period of time that she started receiving hostile letters and telephone calls from a man. After awhile she realized that the individual who was focused on her, had previously been writing and calling her husband when he served as State Chair for the Iowa Democratic Party.

She didn't know what this man wanted or why he had targeted them. His comments to her husband had been political but his comments to her were both political and sexual. For example, the stalker stabbed through a caricature of her on a political flyer; in addition, the mailer, contained threatening and sexually violent comments. The stalker called the Campbell's, wrote them and continued the harassment by having letters mailed to her campaign office and Attorney General's office.

This obscure stalker would also follow them from time to time. On a number of occasions the stalker would call and indicate that he had been where they had been earlier in the day: a political event, the grocery store or a restaurant. Frighteningly, the intimidating stalker let on that he had even been close enough to hear quiet private conversations between her and her husband. She thought his intent was to intimidate and frighten them.

Eventually, Bonnie quit going anywhere alone. She and her husband moved to a secure condominium so that they could feel safe when at home. They became suspicious that the stalker might be a friend because he knew of their daily patterns.

At her swearing in ceremony, when Bonnie became Attorney General, her husband asked the US Attorney if any action could be taken against the stalker. The US Attorney contacted the FBI who eventually located the stalker.

With determination, Attorney General Bonnie Campbell wrote the Iowa anti-stalking law because she became aware that most victims of stalking had no legal remedy. She says that the anti-stalking laws are important to the safety of stalking victims and they reflect a new way of looking at threatening behavior.

She was fortunate, because her position entitled her protection by a federal statute, because the offender used the US Postal Service against a federal officer. However, though her stalker was found,

Bonnie Campbell, decided not to ask the U.S. Attorney to prosecute her stalker because her case was not a strong one. She told me candidly, that she was concerned that the people of Iowa, who just elected her Attorney General, would view her negatively if the prosecution were not successful.

As the highest legal authority in Iowa, Bonnie Campbell gives this advice: "I advise victims of stalking to contact the police immediately. Also, victims should keep a journal of contacts by the stalker. The police can advise whether a protective order might be possible or useful. Most importantly, stalking victims must understand stalking for the serious threat that it is and take every precaution to ensure their safety. Most stalking arises out of intimate relationships, and the evidence is clear that these behaviors are extremely volatile and dangerous, and they must be treated as such".[34]

Another type of stranger stalking which is not uncommon, involves the stalking of a juvenile. One case in particular happened in the Midwest, where a 14-year-old girl, Kathy, was stalked by a 27-year-old male. She didn't he know existed until he began calling her. He called her home a number of times. She thought it was someone from school because he'd describe the clothes she had worn to school. She didn't know what he wanted and at first she didn't feel threatened.

The stalker had noticed Kathy due to her name being in the newspaper because she had played sports at school. His first forms of contact to her were notes, cards, and flowers. Thinking that they were from a classmate, she was flattered. Therefore, she didn't tell her parents about him at first. The cards and letters, he sent were signed with his name or an alias.

During one phone call the stalker told Kathy he would be at her baseball game and he would be wearing a certain type of jacket. She knew she had a problem when during her game she looked up and saw an "older" man wearing the jacket he had described.

As time went on, the phone calls became obscene. He said "gross things" to her. After a while as the calls progressed she thought he was "weird" and told him to leave her alone. When he called and made obscene comments to her she would never respond to him. The "telephone stalking" escalated to 30-35 calls a day. Kathy told her parents, who went to the police. However, the police couldn't do much to help. It was found out later that her stalker was stalking a number of other young women in the surrounding cities. Kathy's family had documented all the calls and got caller ID. Her stalker was finally caught and sentenced to jail. Still, the stalking didn't stop! He actually used the jail phone to continue to stalk her!

Ultimately, Kathy's stalker was sentenced to 2 ½ to 5 years in prison. However, it didn't end there. Though the sentence was punishment for the affliction caused, he continued to phone other victims from prison! During a radio interview, a prison official was asked how such a thing could have happened. The official responded by saying that some judges consider phone usage as a right not a privilege.

Eventually, restrictions on who he could call were made. Kathy was glad he received prison time, however, she didn't think he received enough time for all the terror that he put his victims through.

The stalking had disrupted Kathy's life. For three years, stalking, parental frustration with the authorities, and fear, enveloped this young girl. She didn't feel safe and took a car phone with her. It affected her family's lives. Her parents were frustrated that more couldn't be done to stop the stalker and her sister was always looking behind them.

Kathy says that stalking can happen to anyone. Her advice to her peers is to inform their parents at once, if they are subjected to such offense. Tell their parents right away, and don't hold it in. She was able to survive this because of the love and support of her family and friends. She thinks that she is a strong person and doesn't want someone to take control of her life.

She cautions against talking to strangers, either in one's generation or not. She wants other kids to know that it is not their fault. They did not cause this to happen. When asked if in retrospect, if she knew this was going to happen would she not go into sports. She said that she enjoyed sports and that "No", she didn't want to be stopped from doing something she really liked.
Sports prominence was not the enemy; the stalker was.

In some cases the stalker believes they "can make the person love them". They don't respond to threats of any kind, including violent ones. They may attempt to murder the victim and themselves to link themselves and the victim together forever. Kathy's stalker sent letters saying their destiny was to be together-forever.

In 1990, Los Angeles police department developed its Threat Management Unit to specifically deal with stalking crimes. The following are the results of a study they did, pertaining to erotomanic and love obsession stalkers. The study involved an analysis of 74 cases. In this study, 9 ½% of the stalking cases were categorized as erotomanic. In their overall study, they found the majority of their victims to be female and the majority of stalkers to be male; however in the erotomanic group, 86% of the stalkers were women obsessed with mostly male victims. The study also detected that visits to the victims' home, letter writing and telephone calls were common ways the stalker pursued, his victim. One positive discovery was that 71% of the erotomanic stalkers actually found out where the victim lived, but only a few actually attempted to make contact.

The Threat Management Unit found that while some stalkers suffered from delusional disorders, such as schizophrenia, others didn't suffer from delusions. They just loved their victims in a fanatical obsessive way. 43% of the stalking cases they studied were love obsessional stalkers. Obsessions can last up to thirteen years for love obsession and erotomanic stalkers. Ten months was the average contact for the love obsessional stalker. The erotomanics stalked their victims for twice as long: nineteen months was the average.

WHY DO PEOPLE STALK?
The research that is being compiled on stalking is starting to reveal why one person would stalk someone else. Common reasons include fear of abandonment and fear of rejection. The stalker doesn't want to lose the victim. Therefore, he intimidates-by verbal or physical abuse-the prey, who, he feels, must never be away from his dominance. Also, the stalker may want to "teach the victim a lesson" for leaving him.

Power is another reason. The stalker wants to keep the victim dependent upon them. The stalker will try to keep the victim submissive. Weapons can be used to intimidate a victim. Using intimidation gives the stalker a sense of power - when in actuality he feels as if he holds no power. In this instance, a stalker sends the message- "If you think you can ignore me-think again."

An example of this type of stalking involved a female psychologist, Elizabeth, who dated a very attractive male, Mike, who she met through her church. At first he was very charming and attentive, but after a few months, she lost interest in him. Mike pursued her by phone calls and letters. He even broke into her home and stole personal items and phone directories. When Elizabeth went to church, the stalker was there. She explained her alarming situation to her priest, but the priest was unable to help. He explained that in good conscience, he could not turn anyone away from the church.

She knew Mike was there to stalk her. She needed to get away and decided to go on vacation with friends. She didn't know exactly where they were going to stay. When they decided on a hotel and registered, there was a message waiting for her. It read, "Do you really think I couldn't find you?"

As time went on she pressed charges against the stalker. He in turn pressed charges against her. She knew that he was trying to control her and stay in her life by using the court system.
Elizabeth was flabbergasted that she ignored "stalking clues" that she should have seen because of her training.

It doesn't seem to matter how educated or intelligent people are, many of us don't see the potential trouble because of our needs at the time. Regardless of that, the fault lies with the stalker, not with the victim. Therefore, the victim must quit such a "role" immediately if the stalker is to be stopped.

The world of the stalker is filled with dependency, insecurity, rage and fear of losing the prey. Problems arise when a stalker becomes emotionally attached to the victim, but the victim wants to dissolve the attachment. They become so attached that trying to detach may result in a stalker expressing resentment and rage. This may be because the victim has become the heart of the stalkers world. Trying to detach what matters the most to the stalker, brings out much of the stalker's fear and desperation. The stalker blames others for the detachment and for the consequences for his own actions. Because the stalker blames others for the situation, they may stalk out of revenge.

Along the lines of blaming the victim, Kienlen proposed that psychosocial stressors and recent losses may have an impact on a stalker's behavior. "They experienced the breakup of an intimate relationship or marriage (48%), terminated employment (48%), potential loss of a child (i.e., custody battles, restricted visitation, questioned paternity) (28%), or potential loss of a parent who was seriously ill (8%)". [35]

Stalking may escalate when there is an internal sense of losing control of the victim. " The primary motivation for stalking is not sexual, but is, instead, conscious anger or hostility toward the victim (Meloy, 1996); the most commonly *perceived* motivation for stalking by victims of stalking is control (Tjaden & Thoennes, 1997). [36] When the victim evades the stalker, the stalker may resort to violence.

Another theory is that some stalkers had failed in social or sexual relationships as young adults. "Chronic failures in social or sexual relationships through young adulthood may be a necessary predisposing experience for obsessional followers,' said Reid Meloy, an associate clinical professor of psychiatry at the University of California at San Diego. "In fact, failed relationships are the rule among these individuals." [37]

Even though there is no one set profile of a stalker, Meloy theorizes that obsessional followers do have common variables. These include:

· "a male in his mid-thirties;

· a psychiatric and criminal history;

· a chronic history of failed heterosexual relationships;

· unemployment or underemployment;

· a higher level of intelligence than other offenders;

· has had numerous contacts with his female victim;

· pursues his victim for several months or several years; and

· has made threats, but is usually not physically violent."[38]

Meloy also theorizes that approximately half of them don't even make threats. "The homicide frequency for obsessional followers is below 2 percent. When violence does occur, it is usually committed without a weapon with most victims being pushed, hit, grabbed or fondled." [39]

According to Meloy, in most of the cases which involved obsessional following, the victim was of the opposite sex of the stalker. There were a small number of reported cases in gay and lesbian groups. However, there has not been extensive research in this area.

During my research, I had learned that there were same sex stalkings of disc jockeys in Detroit. One stalker continued to stalk a male DJ, even though the DJ wasn't homosexual. The stalker would call up and make sexually explicit comments to the DJ and also make kissing sounds over the phone. The DJ for personal reasons did not wish to make his story known.

A survey was conducted by the National Institute of Justice and the National Center for Injury Prevention and Control. Included in the survey were statistics concerning stalking victims. It was discovered that men seemed to be stalked by acquaintances and strangers, ninety percent of which were male.

Though men are reluctant to talk of their stalkers, high profiled celebrities, such as Stephen Spielberg whose family life was disrupted by a lone pursuer, have come forward. His case may provide the attention needed to illustrate that men can be stalked and need help. The crime of stalking has effected him and his family.

A 31-year-old man named Jonathan Norman stalked Steven Spielberg. Norman was sexually obsessed with Spielberg. In 1997, Norman was arrested outside Spielberg's home and had in his possession a "rape kit". This kit included razor blades, duct tape, handcuffs and an Exacto knife. He also had a day planner that had the names of Spielberg's family in it. "The planner also contained a cut-out photo of Spielberg's head glued to the body of a younger man, as well a laundry list of items that Norman allegedly planned to use during the attack, including eye masks, dog collars, nipple clamps, chloroform, and a stun gun". [40]

Norman eventually was sentenced to 25 years in prison, due to California's 'three-strikes-and-you're-out-law'. He had been convicted of 2 felonies, resulting from an attempt to run down some pedestrians with his car!

Norman's attorney stated that Norman was a "deluded fan", and tried to get him a lower sentence.

Celebrities became even more worried about their safety when a list of celebrity names, addresses and phone numbers was stolen from the Academy of Television, Arts and Sciences. Apparently, a mass mailing company had possession of the list. A judge ordered the immediate return of the list.

Also, men who are in authoritative positions are stalked. Members of Congress, managers, supervisors and even policemen are at risk.

In one case, Todd, who was employed in a security position, was being stalked by a female co-worker. It started out as flattering attention. In the beginning Todd, liked the attention. The co-worker innocently flirted with him. As time went on the co-worker began to describe the sexy lingerie she was wearing and the sexual favors she wanted to give. Becoming uncomfortable with such talk, Todd asked her to stop, because he was dating another female co-worker at this time. She refused. The stalker would try to cause trouble between the two by telling the girlfriend that Todd really wanted the stalker. Todd told his superiors about the problem, but they acted as if it were a trivial problem. When the stalker started to threaten Todd, he once again voiced his concern. Todd said that since he was male, the beaucracy didn't take his problem seriously, even though he was in fear of the stalker. Eventually the stalker was fired because of poor performance. To make this case even more dispiriting, the woman returned to the workplace, with her boyfriend, who verbally threatened and then attacked Todd. The police were called and the boyfriend was taken away. Todd eventually found other employment in a governmental position.

Another theory on stalking behavior deals with disturbed childhood experiences. "Kienlen et al. (1997) theorized that disturbed childhood experiences such as separation from a primary caregiver, abuse by a parent, or emotional absence of a parent due to mental illness or substance abuse might contribute to the development of a preoccupied attachment pattern in adulthood (Bartholomew, 1990) and ultimately to stalking behavior. [41]

Dr. Gary Kaufmann also, presented an interesting theory on stalking behavior. According to Dr. Kaufmann, stalkers are not assertive within their relationships. I thought that stalking behavior appeared to be very assertive. According to Dr. Kaufmann, the stalker is not assertive when they start stalking. He explains that the *assertion* is isolated in that behavior: "Stalking is really not an assertive response. It is passive aggressive kind of response. The stalker is protected from a reaction by the person who is being stalked. The stalker remains behind the scenes, somewhat protected, while they engage in surveillance or approach at unexpected times giving them the element of surprise. They always have the advantage. Having the advantage requires them not having to be assertive. The aggressive act is not considered assertive. An example, setting fires. Setting a fire is aggressive and destructive. However, perpetrators do it in an unassertive way. They are "in the woodwork" when they do it. No one knows who has done it. They do it in a surreptitious fashion. The effects of it are aggressive."[42]

Those who are unassertive, appear pleasant and selfless. It looks like they try to get along with everyone and tends to put everyone else's needs before their own. "So people in relationships with them really like them. Because if you are in a relationship with this person, your needs come first and that's attractive and part of the seduction."[43]

"At the same time the stalker can be controlling, but in a charming way. The woman may say this guy is perfect. This is almost a red flag. If you look at someone, step back and take an objective view. Something is amiss here. This is not a human being who has typical frailties of a human being-good and bad characteristics." [44]

This person comes across as being absolutely perfect. However, in many cases stalkers don't have social skills. But because they seem perfect and depending upon the victim's needs at the time, the victim often ignores this red flag. Stalkers are very manipulative. "There is suggestive research that stalkers are more intelligent than other criminals, perhaps accounting for their manipulative skills." [45] Once they are involved in the relationship some of that perfection becomes a bit tarnished. Especially, if the woman asserts her own needs in the relationship.

HUNTING THEIR PREY
Stalkers hunt their victims in many ways. The most common way is through telephone calls. As shown earlier, they send gifts, notes flowers and cards as inducements for their prey. Sometimes, 'The Most Dangerous Game' syndrome is sinisterly, affected: The stalker dresses in hunting apparel and follows and pursues his victim as if

they were actually hunting an animal. Carol's stalker was dressed in hunting apparel. Aristotle once said that art imitated life. More than two thousand years later, the philosopher is still right!

Here are other ways that people are stalked. The stalker will:

1. Follow or be wherever the victim is. Intimidation and control are seen here. They may try to control the victim's movements. The victim may not go where they want to go. Intimidation in the respect that no matter where the victim goes the stalker shows up.

2. Persistently approach or come into contact with the victim wherever they are at. Victims have claimed that they are always looking over their shoulder in fear that the stalker will show up.

3. Lurking on the victim's property. This can be very frightening and intimidating for the victim. They never know when the stalker will appear.

4. Continually showing up at the victim's home or work. We know that the workplace is where the stalker knows the victim will be. Sometimes no matter what precautions are taken the stalker still finds a way to get to the victim. The same goes for a victim's home. The stalker knows the victim has to eventually go home. This is the shuddering reality about the crime.

91

5. Persistently contacting the victim by phone or electronic mail. The stalker will contact the victim any way he can.

Even though every case is unique and activities in the cases can vary, there are behaviors that stalkers express that can be seen time and time again. The question is can we predict when violence will occur. Yes, we can. "Violence is a process, as well as an act. Violent behavior does not occur in a vacuum. Careful analysis of violent incidents shows that violent acts often are the culmination of long-developing, identifiable trails of problems, conflict, disputes, and failures."[46]

When violence does occur, we think that we couldn't have foreseen it. Gavin DeBecker an expert on violent behavior, developed a theory called "JACA" to help predict violent behavior. The initials stand for the following:

"PERCEIVED JUSTIFICATION (J) does the person feel justified in using violence?

PERCEIVED ALTERNATIVES (A) Does the person perceive that he has available alternatives to violence that will move him toward the outcome he wants? Since violence, like any behavior, has a purpose, it's valuable to know the goal of the actor.

PERCEIVED CONSEQUENCES (C) How does the person view the consequences associated with using violence? Before resorting to force, people weigh the likely consequences, even if unconsciously or very quickly.

PERCEIVED ABILITY (A) Does the person believe he can

successfully deliver the blows or bullet or bomb? People who have successfully used violence in the past have a higher appraisal of their ability to prevail using violence again." [47]

This theory may help the reader to foresee the occurrence of violent behavior.

CHAPTER 5
STALKING AND THE LAW

Since its conception, many criminal justice professionals are learning more and more on how to deal with stalking situations. As we've seen, some police response has been negative. However, many victims have reported being satisfied with the response that they received. "About half of the victims who had reported to the police were satisfied with the response they received. Victims rated the courts slightly higher--with 60 percent satisfaction. When asked how their situation changed after they reported to the police, about half noted improvement. When asked what the police could have done better, 42 percent said the police should have put their assailant in jail, 16 percent indicated a need to be better protected by the police, and 20 percent said the police should have taken their situation more seriously."[48] Though improvement is needed, overall, it appears that many victims are being helped, which is encouraging.

The stalking laws were made to help individuals who are being stalked. Do they work? The answer to that depends on the criminal justice official handling the case. Not everyone knows about stalking or its ramifications. Depending upon the department and the individual officer, will determine if the stalking law will work for the victim. Some officers take a stalking case very seriously, others may not. One reason why police may not take it seriously, is because of sentences issued by judges. In Robert L. Snow's book, *Stopping A Stalker*, he suggests several reasons why police may not take it seriously. One reason has to do with sentencing. "Also, police officers didn't want to become deeply involved in stalking cases because even when they made an arrest and the prosecutor pressed charges, judges seldom meted out any significant sentences to those found guilty" [49] We've seen some judges who have interpreted the stalking situation as two people who can't get along. Others may see it for what it is-an act of terror often leading to violence.

The stalking law is a good law and a necessary one. As Wayne County Assistant Prosecutor, Nancy Diehl, explains, "I think that right now the laws we have are strong enough. I think they've given us good tools to go forward. I think the laws are there. We have to make sure though, that they are enforced. They are enforced as they should be, through law enforcement and at the prosecutor's office and the courts."[50]

Antistalking laws help law enforcement in their response to stalking cases. However, the laws have certain requirements. It must be proven in seven states, that the stalker intended to cause alarm or annoyance. Some states specifically indicate the number of acts that constitute stalking behavior. "Illinois refers to "acts done on at least two occasions..."; Michigan specifies a "series of two or more separate, noncontinuous acts"; Oklahoma, "two or more separate acts"; and Colorado and North Carolina, "on more than one occasion". [51]

"Two states (Colorado and New Mexico) require the stalker to make a threat and then engage in additional conduct in furtherance of the threat". [52] A victim may feel threatened when the stalker follows the person to work, home or school. All locations seem open to their schemes, as we've seen.

Even though people have been stalked since there have been interactions between people, it took California to lead the way in drafting the first stalking law.

"The California law was drafted after five Orange county women were killed in a six week period in early 1990. All but one had sought help in vain from authorities" [53]

By 1992, twenty-seven states had enacted legislation similar to that of California. Now all fifty states have enacted some form of stalking law. "The new laws aim at halting a pattern of threats and harassment that often precedes violent acts, from assault to rape, child molestation and murder". [54]

"In California, both criminal and civil laws address stalking. According to the criminal laws, a stalker is someone who willfully, maliciously and repeatedly follows or harasses another (victim) and who makes a credible threat with the intent to place the victim or victim's immediate family in fear for their safety. The victim does not have to prove that the stalker had the intent to carry out the threat. (California Penal Code 646.9)"[55]

In Michigan the stalking law states that stalking is: "a '*willful course of conduct*' which involves the repeated or continued harassment of an individual, which would cause a reasonable person to feel terrorized, frightened, intimidated, threatened, '*harassed*', or molested, and actually causes the person to feel terrorized, frightened intimidated, threatened, harassed, or molested."[56]
Also, in Michigan the victim can sue the stalker for damages once the stalker is convicted.

Many states have classifications for stalking. "Many states have both misdemeanor and felony classifications for stalking. Misdemeanors generally carry a jail sentence of up to 1 year. Sentences from 3 to 5 years are typical for felony stalking offenses. Most State statutes contain sentence-enhancing provisions if one or more additional elements are present-for example, if the defendant brandished a weapon, violated a protective order, had committed a prior stalking offense (in 14 States, the prior offense must involve the same victim), or directed his conduct toward a child. Some States allow incarceration for as long as ten years for repeat offenses." [57]

The penalties for stalking and aggravated stalking may vary by state. In Michigan stalking is considered a high misdemeanor. The penalty if convicted is: up to one year in prison and/or up to $1000 in fines and if probation is imposed up to 5 yrs. Aggravated stalking is a more serious offense. It's considered a felony.

A person is guilty of aggravated stalking if:

1. a threat of injury is made to the victim or someone in the victims household
2. the person violates an anti-stalking PPO, a condition of bond, probation or pre-trial release
3. the person had a previous conviction for stalking.

The punishment for aggravated stalking can be imprisonment of up to 5 yrs and/or a fine of up to $10,000. Probation may be given for a period of not less then 5 yrs.

In Indiana and Missouri, the crime is elevated to aggravated stalking, if it can be proven that the stalker intended to cause fear.

"Four states require that a threat be made to prove aggravated stalking, but not stalking. Statutes in Hawaii and Texas prohibit threats in conjunction with intent to damage property and threats in conjunction with intent to cause personal injury". [58]

California's anti-stalking penalties are as follows:
"The criminal penalty for stalking is imprisonment up to a year and/or a fine of up to $1,000. There are more severe penalties when the stalker pursues the same person in violation of a court restraining order, with a sentencing range of two to four years imprisonment. Persons convicted of felony stalking also face stricter penalties if they continue to stalk their victim(s). Courts may issue restraining orders to prohibit stalking.(California Family Code 6320)" [59]

When we talk about stalking and the law, we need to mention personal protection orders. This is an order by the court that states that the stalker must have no contact with the victim. If the PPO is violated, criminal penalties can result. They are there to help protect the victim and help the police in enforcing the anti-stalking law. It gives the police the right to arrest the stalker if the PPO is violated.

A PPO can be obtained at the county clerk's office or the local circuit court in the victim's county. An attorney may not be needed. There also may not be a fee but the victim needs to check with the court. It's a proactive weapon that can be used if the victim goes to court. It shows that the victim was concerned and felt threatened. They were developed to protect people from real threats. However, PPO's are being misused. According to Sen. William Van Regenmoter, chairman of the Senate Judiciary Committee and sponsor of the legislation, there are plans in the works to tighten its scope. "No way did I envision that it would be used in the context that some people are using it," he said, "But the bottom line is that judges still have to make decisions." [60]

The problem with PPO's has to do with people manipulating them for revenge purposes. Police departments are cluttered with PPO's that involve an ex-spouse trying to get back at the other spouse for whatever reason; or neighbors filing a PPO against another neighbor because of problems with pets. Also, filed are PPO's, which involved spats between girlfriends over boyfriends. One case involved two elderly women who conflicted when one caught the other feeding birds on her lawn. "In Macomb County, two 13-year-old Sterling Heights boys appeared in court last February when one obtained a PPO against the other because of fights. A judge threatened both with juvenile detention if they didn't steer clear of each other. The county had a similar case weeks earlier, involving two 10-year-old girls, who also couldn't stop squabbling."[61] This misuse of PPO 's takes the police away from cases that are really in need of their help and protection.

In Michigan there are no statistics that show how many PPO's are violated. However, the Women's Survival Center of Oakland County had estimated that of the PPO's issued between August 1997 and December 1997 13 % were ignored.

To give you an idea of the number of personal protection orders granted, the following is a chart that shows the number of orders granted in three counties of Metro Detroit.

Seeking protection

Figures show personal protection orders granted in Metro Detroit's three counties since 1995, through June this year

	Wayne	Oakland	Macomb
1995	5,289	2,961	445
1996	8,366	3,614	2,217
1997	10,254	3,171	2,231
Mid-1998	8,000	2,023	1,471

Source: Circuit court administrator in each county [62]

100

There is some confusion about protection orders. There are PPO's, restraining orders or injunctions and "no contact" or stay orders. Restraining orders are generated by the victim and filed for in civil court. No contact orders are generated by judges as conditions of bond or probation. According to Nancy Diehl, "Personal protection orders, restraining orders and injunction orders are the same. It is to show the victim that there is help for them...." [63] In Michigan the personal protection order is in effect for 182 days. In California, Temporary Restraining Orders which are also called TRO's, are in effect for 14 days. To determine if the order will be extended, the victim must return to court for a trial. In Michigan a small percentage of PPO's are rejected. "Only about 10 percent of PPO requests are rejected, out of the more than 15,000 sought each year in Wayne, Oakland and Macomb counties."[64]

At one point, some states were looking to enact legislation that made it mandatory for judges to go through PPO training. There was a concern that some judges didn't read the PPO's before signing them; they had their clerks sign them.

In the cases that I have researched, PPO's did not stop the stalkers behavior. If anything, PPO's increased the stalker's behavior or complicated the situation. Many stalkers are not concerned about the law. They feel that murdering their victim is justified. They were not in the least deterred by these orders. Defendants feel that the victim belongs to them and they can do whatever they feel is necessary to accomplish their goal. In domestic violence cases, as with stalking, just because someone may face imprisonment, that may not deter them. "Lynn McCaully knows the emotion. She endured seven years of black eyes, busted lips and verbal abuse before seeking a PPO against her husband. Now the Westland mother finds herself sharing a category that increasingly includes matters like wayward pets. She remains on the run from her ex-husband, hole up in HAVEN, a Pontiac shelter for battered women. She has a PPO, but it never kept her ex-husband away-despite possible contempt penalties that include 93 days in jail and a $500 fine.[65]

However, PPO's can help, because if the stalker violates it, a case can be built against the stalker. It gives the police grounds to act quickly. Susan explained it very well when she said that the PPO didn't stop her stalker, but gave her the paper trail which ultimately got her help. It is important to remember that a PPO can cause a false sense of security or safety. One must keep in mind that PPO's do help in some cases. In others, if the stalker feels he owns the person, nothing will stop him from attempting to do whatever he wants to do to the victim. "The same court order used on an estranged husband asks him to abandon, at the stroke of a judge's signature, the central features of his life: his intimate relationship, his control and ownership of another human being, his identity as a powerful man, his identity as a husband, and on and on." [66]

"In fact, so many victims under orders of protection were being killed that we came to refer to the court orders as "orders of illusion." These documents gave the victim the illusion of being protected but were virtually unenforceable."[67] Victims need to use their own judgment on whether to file or not. Sometimes the stalking will stop if a PPO is filed. Other times the stalking will escalate to violence, even death, if a PPO is filed.

This can be seen in the case of Laura Black. A co-worker asked her out, but she declined. The co-worker, Richard Farley, would not accept the fact that she did not want to go out with him. The company that they worked for, told him stop bothering her but his harassment only escalated. He eventually made death threats to her.

Laura did file a restraining order against Richard. Eventually, Richard was fired from his job. One day, he returned to the company carrying several weapons: handguns, shotguns and a rifle. He shot ten employees. He found Laura and shot her with the rifle. She lay on the floor bleeding, but eventually crawled out of the building. Seven of the ten died. Farley went on this rampage the day before he and Laura were to appear in court to make the temporary restraining order permanent. Laura wasn't comfortable about filing the restraining order. Her company however, advised her to, saying that if she didn't file, that it might have an impact on any future promotion opportunities. "Her intuition about him was right on the mark when she told the court, "I am afraid of what this man might do to me if I file this action."[68]

CONSTITUTIONAL ISSUES

When stalking laws were first developed, the laws covered a broad range of behaviors. Because the range of behaviors was so extensive, there was a concern that constitutional protections were being violated. Many of the early stalking statutes that were initially developed were constitutionally attacked for this reason. A few lower courts even condemned these laws.

Clearly there was a problem, so lawmakers had to amend their stalking statutes in order to correct any constitutional weaknesses. A model stalking statute was developed. It was refined by The National

Criminal Justice Association, in conjunction with the National Institute of Justice and the National Victim Center. Victims, criminal justice organizations and experts also contributed to the statute. The model language makes it a crime to: "Engage in a course of conduct that would place a reasonable person in fear for their safety, and that the stalker intended and did, in fact, place the victim in such fear." [69]

We know that individuals who are involved in stalking situations go through wracking inordinate ordeals that no one should have to go through. They are not to blame. The stalker is the party who should be held completely responsible. However, when a stalker is charged with stalking, many times the stalking statutes are challenged. It is unbelievable that the stalker would have any power to challenge the stalking statutes, however it has happened. The problem lies in the difference between what is considered lawful activity and what is considered stalking activity.

People accused of stalking have challenged that the laws are vague under due process principles. A case that characterizes this is People v. Holt.

"In *People* v. *Holt*,19 for example, the defendant was convicted under the Illinois antistalking law for repeatedly showing up at the local skating rink where his former girlfriend took private skating lessons and watching her during her lessons even though there was a restraining order against him. The Illinois statute provides that "a person commits stalking when he or she, knowingly and without lawful justification, on at least two separate occasions, follows another person or places the person under surveillance or any combination thereof and...places that person in reasonable apprehension of immediate or future bodily harm, sexual assault, confinement or restraint," 20 In rejecting the defendant's vagueness claim and upholding the statute, the court concluded that it "adequately warns innocent persons of the conduct to be avoided: making threats, following, or placing someone under surveillance, and thereby reasonably producing intimidation, apprehension and fear." 21 The law does not rely on strictly subjective standards, but rather: sets explicit, objective standards for defendant's actions, knowledge, and the effect of his conduct on his victim."22 [70]

It is encouraging to note that it is rare for a court to condemn antistalking statutes on the grounds of vagueness.

A second challenge claims that antistalking laws may be unconstitutionally overbroad when they deal with activity protected by the first amendment. "An antistalking statute will be found to be unconstitutionally overbroad where it reaches activity protected by the first Amendment, including the exercise of free speech or lawful assembly"[71]

There have been several overbreadth challenges to antistalking statutes, but the courts have upheld their decisions. A case that illustrates this is People v. White

In this case, in Michigan, the defendant was accused of calling his former girlfriend as much as 100 times a week. He called her at home, at work, showed up at her work and threatened her and her family. He plead guilty and was convicted of attempted aggravated assault. He wanted to get his conviction overturned.

"The defendant sought to overturn his conviction, arguing that the statute unconstitutionally abridged his First Amendment right to speech by permitting a complainant to subjectively determine which telephone calls are acceptable and which are criminal.

The court did not agree. In upholding the statute, the court remarked, "Defendant's repeated telephone calls to the victim, sometimes 50 to 60 times a day whether the victim was at home or at work, and his verbal threats to kill her and her family do not constitute protected speech or conduct serving a legitimate purpose, even if that purpose is 'to attempt to reconcile,' as defendant asserts." 28 The aim of the law is to prevent such activity because the threat of violence, which is almost always present in these types of cases, may eventually result in the death of the victim. 20[72] Nineteen states have been challenged on constitutional concerns.

Many states have amended their initial laws since the early 1990's when the first antistalking legislation had been passed. This was due to a couple of concerns. One of which, as mentioned, concerned constitutional challenges. Another pertained to other issues that came forth when the laws were implemented.

"Many of the initial statutes, for example, did not specifically prohibit threats or assaults on nonfamily members, such as the victim's new intimate partner. In general, the revised laws include specific intent and credible threat requirements, broaden definitions, refine wording, stiffer penalties, and emphasize the suspect's pattern of activity."[73]

There are a wide variety of stalking related provisions. Some state stalking statutes:

> 1. "Allow police to make warrantless arrests in stalking cases where probable cause exists;

2. Make stalking a non-bailable offense under certain circumstances;

3. Provide for automatic and emergency protective orders;

4. Require mandatory psychological evaluation and treatment for stalkers;

5. Establish sentencing enhancements in cases where the victim is a minor, or when there is a protective order in place against the perpetrator; and

6. Create heightened crime classifications for stalkers who commit second stalking offences.[74]

In order to ensure further safety for stalking victims, the Interstate Stalking Punishment and Prevention Act was formed. On February 28, 1996, Rep. Ed Royce, of California introduced the Interstate Stalking Punishment and Prevention Act of 1996. It states,
"Sec. 2261A. Interstate stalking
Whoever travels across a State line or enters or leaves Indian country with the intent to injure or harass another person, and in the course of, or as a result of, such travel places that person in reasonable fear of the death of, or serious bodily injury to, that person or a member of that person's immediate family (as defined in section 115) shall be punished as provided in section 2261"[75] This law protected people from being stalked across state lines.

"The Interstate Stalking Punishment and Prevention Act makes it a federal crime for any stalker to cross state lines to pursue a victim. The Act makes it:

A federal crime whether or not there is a protection order in effect. Before today, women who did not have protection orders, or who did not have an intimate relationship with their stalker, were not protected by federal law. Today's legislation protects them regardless of the prior situation.

A federal crime before any act of violence has been committed. Victims pursued across state lines by a spouse or intimate no longer have to suffer an act of violence before they can be protected by federal resources.[76]

Before the law was passed, if a woman left the state to be safe, she could lose the protection of a restraining order issued by that state. Generally, restraining orders issued in one state are usually not valid in another state. Now a person would be committing a federal crime if they crossed state lines in violation of a restraining order to harass or injure a victim; this would include stalking someone on federal property. Also, the law makes it easier to enforce protection orders across state borders and provides extended protection to the victim's family. Five to twenty years in jail could be imposed for violating the anti-stalking law. Longer jail sentences will be imposed if the violator causes life-threatening injuries or permanently disfigure their victims. The violator will receive life imprisonment should the victim die. Senator Kay Bailey Hutchinson (R. Tex.) and Rep. Ed Royce (R. Cal.) have sponsored this bill.

Federal anti-terrorism laws were also offered to protect victims. "Federal anti-terrorism laws may also apply in some **stalking** cases, allowing victims to bring charges in federal court as an alternative to the state criminal court of their jurisdiction. These laws may also prove useful in **stalking** cases where the offender makes threatening phone calls from outside the state where the victim resides" [77]

CHAPTER 6
HOW TO DEAL WITH A STALKING SITUATION

When a victim is being stalked, they should take the situation seriously. They need to call the police when they feel threatened. However, victims can not always expect the police, judges or prosecutors to have expertise on the crime of stalking. Stalking victims might have to provide police with a copy of their state stalking statute as well as proof that the stalker violated the statute. State statutes can be found in each state's published criminal code. They also may be available at law libraries and some public libraries. Even if there is not sufficient evidence to prove a stalking situation, victims still should file a complaint as soon as possible.

"In some cases, victims may also be able to file a complaint in the jurisdiction where the offender resides, if it is different from the victim's." [78]

If it appears that the police won't investigate or if they do not respond to a complaint, victims can always contact their local prosecutor. Prosecutors are also known as: state's attorney, district attorney or state solicitor. Stalking victims should try to work closely with the prosecutor. In working with the prosecutor, it is essential to explain the problem comprehensively, and have evidence on hand. To help their case, victims need to document every single contact with the stalker. This can't be stressed enough. Document, document, document. Documentation helps the victim to gain credibility and can be used in court as evidence.

The victim needs to decide if they're willing to see the case to its completion. It is very frustrating to prosecutors when a victim is not willing to pursue their case. "A prosecutor's office that feels they have a victim who will stick with the case is much more willing to be aggressive in their prosecution".[79]

If victims receive anything from the stalker, they should be careful not to smear fingerprints in case they need to prove who was doing the stalking. According to Robert L. Snow, "However, don't do as police detectives on television and in the movies do: pick up items with a handkerchief. This is a Hollywood invention. Police officers don't really do that. This will smear fingerprints just as easily as using your bare hands will. Pick up papers by the corners and objects by rough parts that likely couldn't contain fingerprints anyway. Put everything received in clear plastic bags." [80] Some victims have thrown away cards and letters received from the stalker. This is a mistake. Remember, Joan wanted to throw away all the negativity. She didn't, because she knew that one day they may be used as evidence. Keep everything and record all contact. For example, all notes, letters and gifts.

We are all responsible for our own safety. There are steps everyone can take to help protect themselves against a stalker. One step, is to be aware of our surroundings. Another one is that wherever we go, we need to know who is around us and where there is an exit in case we need to use it.

Basic precautions that can be taken are:

1. Call police the moment you feel threatened.
2.Document all contact with the stalker. Keep everything received from the stalker.
3.Give a description of the stalker and his vehicle to the police.
4. Have a camera ready to take pictures of the stalker when he is on your property.
5. Do not contact or meet with the stalker.
6. Do a home security check. Ask your local police department to go over their recommendations.
7. Have a panic button installed near your bed and/or on a key chain.
8. Take safety precautions when you're out.
9. Don't keep the stalking to yourself. Tell family, friends and co-workers.
10.Have an escape plan and kit ready just in case you need to leave in a hurry.
11.Have a safe room installed in your home.
12.Carry pepper spray. Know that pepper sprays may not always be effective. The spray may not work on attackers who are high on drugs or mentally disturbed. Also, attackers may have sprayed themselves with spray and are immune to it.
13.Get a car phone, have it pre-programmed to 911.

*In Provo Utah, five emergency cellular phones were donated by AT&T Wireless Services. The police are lending out cellular phones to victims of stalking and violent crime. The hope is that victims can save themselves with the push of a button. The phones are programmed to dial 911. Once the perpetrator has been arrested or stops stalking the victim, the phones will be returned. "More than half the time we respond to the scene of a domestic-violence incident, the phone has been pulled out of the wall or damaged in some way," said Vicky Proctor, coordinator for the Provo Police Department Victim Assistance program. "If the perpetrator can cut off the victim's communication with others who can help, then he is in control."[81]

The cell phones will also help the police. If the stalker is pursuing the victim by car, the police can be called and arrest the stalker.

Purchasing a hand gun is one option. However, this is an important decision with many implications that must be considered very seriously. The idea of owning a gun may be frightening for some people, while others may feel more secure because of it. One person I interviewed, said he had his rifle attached to the side of his bed. Fear drove this person to the point of doing this. If a victim chooses to own a gun, they need to know how to use it. This would be accomplished through training and practicing at a shooting range. The victim must be able to shoot the gun if they're attacked. If the victim doesn't think they could shoot when attacked-they shouldn't have one. Also, victims should become educated on their states laws concerning handguns. Some states require a permit to carry a concealed weapon, while it's illegal in other states to do so. Keep in mind that any weapon can be taken from the victim and used to hurt them. Guns have even been taken away from police officers. "Between 1983 and 1992, 16 percent of the police officers in the United States killed by handguns were killed with their own gun that had been taken away from them or by a handgun taken away from another police officer"[82]

Another way to deal with a stalking situation is to change your identity. Some stalkers just won't stop. If a victim believes that their life is in jeopardy and they have exhausted other possibilities, changing their identity may be an alternative. It is very difficult for someone to completely disappear. The stalker will use every avenue to locate them. They may even hire a private detective. Private investigators I have spoken with, are concerned when they are requested to locate someone. They ask the client why the investigation is wanted because they don't want to be involved in cases where a stalker is looking to kill a victim.

A case which involved a woman who had to change her identity is Sally's case. Sally was a professional in her field. She married a man who seemed to be the perfect husband. Within two years of marriage however, he went from verbally abusive to physically abusive. They were very well off and had no children. Sally was raped by him and feared for her life. Slowly she started to plan her escape. One day instead of going to work she packed her bags and went to stay with friends. After a while, she was so concerned about the safety of her friends, that she decided for everyone's safety, that she would move into a safehouse. Where once this woman had expensive cars and furs, she was now in a safe house with only a few belongings. She changed her name and moved into a subdivision where no one knew her. She was very careful to cover all of her tracks. She found out later that her husband had abused his other two wives. When she goes out in the morning to get her mail, she waves at her neighbors. They think she's just like them- living their lives safely and happily in a nice little subdivision. When asked what does he want from her- she says he wants to rape and humiliate her. Now he has another girlfriend. She may become wife number four. Sally and the other two wives think that he'll kill number four.

To escape, or in trying to regain control of their world, sometimes

There are precautions victims can take to disappear and protect themselves, but keep in mind, they will have to always be on their guard. "Stalkers have been known to travel thousands of miles and spend thousands of dollars in pursuit of their victims, and the smallest slip-up in your new identity can undo it all". [83]

The steps that can be taken:
1. Have an unpublished and unlisted phone number
2. U.S. Postal Service –file a change of address card. Give only a few friends the residential address.
3. Post office box- don't use your address on any correspondence. Use a private post office box. It can be listed as "Suite 120" or "Apartment 120".
For additional security, acquire several post office boxes in different cities and locations.

Beware of any large packages that aren't expected that are brightly wrapped. The stalker can wait and see who picks it up and follow it to the victim. Not only will this put the victim in jeopardy, but also whoever picks it up.

Another way is to use a mail drop. A mail drop is a rented address. It's a service that will let the victim use their address for a fee. Check the yellow pages under the titles of mail forwarding services or mailing services. There is a book which has a listing of over 700 mail drops for the United States and Canada. It's called: *The Directory of Mail Drops*, by Michael Hoy.

4. Use Caller ID to help screen calls. There are special codes to ensure that your phone number is not disclosed. Check with your

4. Use Caller ID to help screen calls. There are special codes to ensure that your phone number is not disclosed. Check with your phone company to see what is available for you.

5. Use an answering service-This is a service where an operator will handle all your incoming calls.

6. Financial Institutions-use a friend or relatives name to open a new account. The reason to do this is that stalkers can call the bank under some pretense and find out your address and phone number.

7. Credit Card Companies-Alert them to your situation. Request that they "flag" your record and notify you of any access.

8. Magazines-cancel any subscriptions that disclose your address.

9. Social Security Number-don't reveal it on your checks. Only give it out if you absolutely have to. Never give it out over the phone.

10. Internet-Don't reveal personal information on online computer services.

11. Government Agencies-Some government agency records are public record.

*A stalker can access information you reveal to that agency. Department of Motor Vehicles and business licenses are among some of these agencies. Check with your DMV to see how address information can be confidential.

Changing one's identity may be the way to go. It may be the way the victim has to go to stay alive. Each case has to be evaluated for risk and safety.

The following chart gives some perspective on protection measures people have taken. [84]

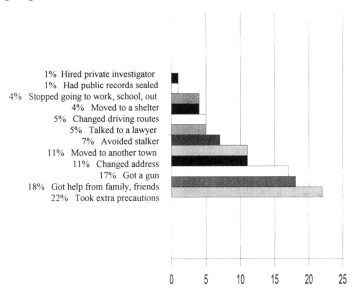

1%	Hired private investigator
1%	Had public records sealed
4%	Stopped going to work, school, out
4%	Moved to a shelter
5%	Changed driving routes
5%	Talked to a lawyer
7%	Avoided stalker
11%	Moved to another town
11%	Changed address
17%	Got a gun
18%	Got help from family, friends
22%	Took extra precautions

A stalker may be able to find the victim if they aren't careful in handling some of the steps mentioned. Another way to locate people is through the Internet. There are websites on the Internet that allows access to telephone books across the country. The Internet also gives access to brokers, who for a price will find out any information that an individual wants them to. If someone had access to a victim's social security number, they could find out information on where to find the victim. He may tap into all of the victim's personal, financial and professional records! Unfortunately, with the development of the Internet, many privacy problems have been created for the sake of speed.

Unless victims take methodical steps to protect themselves, for a price someone may be able to locate them. The following information from Michael Scott's, *HOW TO LOSE ANYONE ANYWHERE,* demonstrates how much it may cost to obtain information on someone.

"**Unlisted Phone Numbers**: You give a PI a phone number, listed or not listed, and for approximately $45.00 you can get the address. If you have the town and no street address but want the phone number, that's available for $75.00. Usually takes about two days.

Utility Information: Give an information broker someone's name, and city and state, and Utility information can be bought for $60.00- you get the address/place of employment listed on application/ relative information.

Social Security Administration: There are some individuals who have sources at the SSA. If you are able to have or get a source at the SSA, your wages, place of employment, address, new names used with you ssn, and your children's names are all recorded. This can be bought for anywhere from $50.00 to $400.00.

Post Office Box Inf.: It used to be you could just give the post master $1.25 for a change of address or street address to a PO Box. With the new Domestic Violence laws, you can no longer do this. For $100.00 the address or PO Box information can be bought.

Department of Motor Vehicles: DMV is available for most states for under $20.00. There are some states, California, Missouri, to name a few, that have privacy laws and you can't get the street address. An underground DMV for those private states would usually cost $50.00.

Magazine Subscriptions: For $20.00 you can give an information broker a name and there's a database that has every single person in this country that receives a subscription to a magazine—it will yield every Mary Jane Smith in the USA receiving a subscription, with addresses.[85]

Underground credit reports can also be purchased for $40.00. Credit reports show name, address, phone number, former addresses along with other pertinent information.

ELECTRONIC STALKING: WHAT TO DO IF IT HAPPENS

Another area of concern is electronic stalking. There are many ways of communication today. The Web, Internet and e-mail are being used more and more frequently with other forms of communication developing. They are wonderful tools to be used for the right reasons. However, they can also be used by someone to stalk and hurt others. Just because we can't see or hear a person's voice, doesn't mean that it can't cause us to feel frightened, intimidated or fearful. Stalking over the Internet is a crime and its happening today.

In Michigan, a Dearborn Heights man was convicted of stalking a Farmington Hills woman by using computer messages. He was sentenced to a year's probation and ordered to undergo a psychiatric evaluation. He could have received one year in jail and $1,000 fine.

The two had met through a video dating service, The woman had contacted him. They were both interested in computers. They had spoke on the phone, met twice and communicated through electronic mail messages. After wanting to end the relationship the woman received approximately 20 messages.

When she found out that the man watched her leave work, she called the Farmington Hills police department. The police notified him to stop sending the messages or he'd be arrested. He persisted and was arrested. The woman cut her hair, moved and got a new car. Assistant Oakland County Prosecutor, Neil Rocking, who prosecuted the case stated that computer stalking can't be policed like other crimes. "From the secure privacy of their home, in the glow of a computer, you can stalk somebody," he said. "Detection is very difficult." E-mail stalker sentencing likely will influence future cases.[86]

Another case involves Robert Maynard the CEO of Internet America. Robert Maynard was stalked. His stalker was harassing him in cyberspace and threatening his family.

The stalker's messages were posted on an Internet newsgroup and many ended with the following poem: "Lord, grant me the serenity to accept the things I cannot change…and the wisdom to hide the bodies of the people I had to kill". [87] When the negative communication did not stop, Maynard sought assistance through the court system. He received help through Judge Joe. B. Brown. He was the first person to use e-mail to issue a legal order, in this case a restraining order. The restraining order was issued to stop the stalker from harassing Maynard, his family and employees. Because of the restraining order, the stalker was restricted from using e-mail to harass Maynard. The stalker was also ordered to not be within 500 yards of Maynard's home or business. A hard copy of the restraining order was also presented by the sheriff.

Internet America wrote a code of ethics for its Internet uses. It warns that illegal activities won't be tolerated by the company from anyone who is offensive or disruptive. "The accepted use policy of IA is:

1. Say or do whatever you want in the appropriate forum. If you're not sure what's appropriate, ask.
2. Don't do anything that's illegal in Texas. If illegal content is reported as originating from our system, we will delete the file and report the action to the appropriate victims and/or law enforcement. If illegal content is reported on our system which originated from outside, we will delete the file from public access, archive the item for law enforcement and report the action to the originating system's administrator.
3. Don't do anything to jeopardize the integrity for the Internet of Internet America's systems.
4. Follow generally prescribed Accepted Use policies of the Internet's global community."[88]

There is help available to victims of online stalking and harassment. There is a group called Cyber Angels who gives information on what to do when being stalked on-line.

This organization was founded by the International Alliance of Guardian Angels. This Internet safety organization discovered that many cases of cyberstalking can turn into real-life stalking. "Renee Goodale, executive director of Survivors of Stalking, an anti-stalking resource center, agrees. She says that virtually every case of cyberstalking escalates beyond online terror". [89] They have developed a help page on what can be done to help prevent victims from being stalked.

A few of their ideas with on-line harassment are:

1. " Keep your cool.
2. Remember Silence is Deadly!
3. If you respond and flame them, you are likely to start a flame war.
4. The main thing is to remember that harassers are looking for someone they can intimidate/scare/shock, like the guy who sends a woman an obscene message. Don't give them the pleasure of finding out that you're upset by it!
5. As the one receiving the message, you have the power, not the person sending the message. If you don't reply, the person will get bored and find someone else to bother.
6. But you should remember to save the messages and information from the stalker and give all this information to the authorities. Just because this person isn't bothering you anymore, doesn't mean you want them to be bothering other people.
7. Above all remember that unless this person has your home address, they can not harm you, but it is in your and everyone else's best interest to make certain this person is stopped and convicted."[90]
Similar to physical stalking, if you're being stalked tell the police and others close to you. Don't wait and don't fall into the stalking trap of isolation.

Cyber stalkers are very similar to other stalkers. They can be obsessional and delusional and have low self-esteem and won't take "No" for an answer. These stalkers hunt for prey that can be easily controlled and/or manipulated. Cyberstalkers are educated with their technology and search for victims who lack basic skills and expertise in Internet reporting or complaint procedures.

According to CyberAngels, "Cyberstalkers will also look for places where vulnerable users in the real life sense may be found. If we take four IRC (live chat) channels called #cybersex, #flirts, #romance and #friends, and ask the question: which of these four channels are MORE likely to attract cyberstalkers and which LESS likely, the answers may surprise some readers.

Many people think that the live chat channels that will attract MOST harassment will be the sex channels like #cybersex or #flirts, but in my experience this is not so. Channels like these attract experienced adult "players" who are more likely to be confident with technology and with their own personal communications skills. They are LESS likely to be traumatized for example by sexually explicit messages sent to them by a stranger, and they will be less naïve and trusting too.

In fact the more vulnerable channels are the Romance and Friends channels, and from this environment I have received most of the requests for help and advice. Romance and Friends forums attract a more vulnerable user-people looking for friendship, companionship-and these users are generally not as technically skilled. They are also more likely to be more trusting of strangers as they are less "cyberstreetsmart". Romance and Friends channels then provide the cyberstalker with exactly what he wants- a steady stream of users who fit his target profile." [91]

There are a few of U.S. states that specifically mention Electronic Communications in their anti-stalking statutes.

Those are:

Arizona
Alaska
Connecticut
Michigan
New York
Oklahoma
Wyoming

CHAPTER 7
HOW TO DEAL WITH A STALKER

When a stalking situation has developed, the victim should have *no contact* with the stalker. The victim needs to *clearly* get across the idea that they don't want anything to do with the stalker. Any contact in the stalker's mind is seen as encouragement, even if the victim is hostile towards the stalker. Even when the victim is pushed to her limit and can't stand it any longer and lashes out verbally to the stalker, saying she doesn't want to be bothered any more-the stalker thinks the victim is testing the stalker's love and devotion. The stalker wants a positive reaction, but even if they receive a negative one, at least they are in the victim's life. They want some contact with the victim. Any contact indicates to the stalker, that the victim wants to resume the relationship. When it doesn't happen there's frustration.

When the victim starts dating or gets married to another person, this threatens the relationship the stalker has with the victim. When the victim demonstrates that the relationship is over, violence can result. If from the beginning, there was no contact with the stalker, there is a greater probability that violence will not occur.

In many cases, victims send mixed messages. It doesn't take much behavior on the victim's part for the stalker to interpret their behavior as wanting to reconcile. The victim may think that if they talk to the stalker one more time, he'll go away. In Joan's case, she didn't want to hurt his feelings and thought if she explained the situation, everything would be fine. Of course, this never worked.

125

"Do not negotiate, Once a woman has made the decision that she doesn't want a relationship with a particular man, it needs to be said one time, explicitly. Almost any contact after that rejection will be seen as negotiation. If a woman tells a man over and over again that she doesn't want to talk to him, that is talking to him, and every time she does it, she betrays her resolve in the matter." [92]

Once the victim does talk to the stalker, they realize that it was a bad idea. They shouldn't have made the effort to explain in the hope that the person would just go away and not be mad. It doesn't work. This behavior sets the stalker up to become frenzied. Because of the ambivalence, the stalker is on a "roller coaster ride". To him, she doesn't know what she wants. In the stalker's mind, they know what they want; a response from the victim. If the victim doesn't respond the stalker will continue until he finds what will make the victim respond. For example - the stalker calls 20 times a day for 3 days. The fourth day the victim can't stand it anymore and yells into the phone 'quit calling me'. The stalker now knows that it takes four days and/or 61 calls to get the victim's attention. This could go on for years and years. "If you don't react to the stalker, then the stalker is not able to intimidate and control you, which is what he or she wants and craves."[93]

The victim should never agree to meet with the stalker. Every stalker and stalking situation is unpredictable. The stalker may seem pleasant and rational but could turn violent in an instant. A stalking victim should never underestimate the danger that they are in.

If the victim does contact the stalker, the stalker can turn around and say that the victim is pursuing them. If the victim should try to bring charges against the stalker, the stalker can have counter charges brought against the victim. We've seen this in Tony's case. The stalker can easily turn the tables and make the victim look like the stalker. This can be seen in cases where the stalker leaves love notes and the victim calls and threatens the stalker to leave them alone. The stalker looks like the victim. Outwardly, it looks like he's the one in trouble. Some victims want to beat the stalker at their own game. If the stalker follows them, they start to follow the stalker. Not only is the stalker getting the attention he craves, he can also turn this around and say he's the one being stalked.

At one conference I spoke at, a police officer said that if he were stalked, he would do to the stalker exactly what the stalker did to him. In other words, he would reciprocate in kind. When I explained that he would look like the bad guy, the officer asked why should he go through "hell", while the stalker did whatever he/she wanted to do? The officer couldn't see the ramifications that could occur because of his actions. Number one, as previously mentioned, the stalker wants to be a part of the victim's life, even if it is a negative part. Two, especially being a police officer, a stalker could twist that into the stalker being victimized. The situation could keep the officer in the stalker's life longer and make the police department look bad. If both, officer and department look bad, there will be a negative perception of the police with the community.

Unfortunately, sometimes the stalker may be a police officer. If this is the case, notify the police chief immediately so the problem can be dealt with. If someone is being stalked by a police officer, and files a personal protection order against that officer, in Michigan, the officer may not carry a firearm. If the officer can't carry a firearm, then the officer can't perform routine duties. This has been controversial, because what should be done with an officer who can't carry their firearm? Some departments place the officer on suspension with pay until the situation can be investigated. Other departments allow the officer to work a desk position.

Victims can protect themselves by contacting the police. The police can file a police report. Police can often go a step further. They can send a letter to the stalker, indicating that their behavior must stop. In some situations this might work. They can go see the stalker or have the stalker come to the police station. Confronting the stalker face to face sometimes is effective for some stalkers. However, in many cases, it is not effective. "When police visit him and say, in effect, "Cut this out or you'll get into trouble," the pursuer intuitively knows that if they could have arrested him they would have arrested him. So what's the result of the visit? Well, the greatest possible weapon in his victim's arsenal- sending the police after him- came and went without a problem. The cops stopped by, they talked to him, and they left. Who got stronger, the victim or the pursuer?" [94]

Keep in mind when talking to the police to gather as much information as possible. Stalkers can sound very believable. The police will not know whom to believe at first. Also, if there is a relationship with the stalker, the police should be told the truth to help ensure that the police know the stalker is the problem and not the victim. Whatever relationship (if any) the victim and the stalker have, has no bearing on determining whether to arrest and charge a suspect with stalking. Certain behaviors are prohibited by law regardless if there is a relationship between the victim and stalker.

What can be done to stalkers to keep them away from victims? Incarceration is one solution. It gets the stalker off the street. It may help in some cases but not others. However, at this time convicted stalkers aren't receiving substantial jail, prison or mental facility sentences. "Sitting someone down in jail for a while may make him rethink his actions." But some stalkers are mentally deranged. Stanton Samenow, a Virginia clinical psychologist and author of "Inside the Criminal Mind," says that many have disturbed self-images in which they see themselves as irresistible or complete zeros. When they are rejected, they resort to intimidation in a desperate attempt to try to regain self-esteem. The threat of prison may deter some of them, but for others, says Samenow, "it's like putting fuel on a fire? [95] A number of criminal justice professionals have told me that when a stalker is in jail, it only gives them time to think about what they're going to do to the victim once they get out.

It was astonishing that the juvenile's stalker continued to phone his victims from prison. Steps are being taken to help prevent this from happening in the future. Joyce Quin, the Prisons and Probation Minister, announced that a strategy was developed to help prevent a stalker from contacting a victim from prison. The strategy, 'smart telephone technology' will allow inmates access to pre-approved telephone numbers only and will replace the old card system. Therefore, unauthorized calls will be terminated, while recipients will be notified of the caller before contact is made.

Joyce Quinn states, "It is very important to me that any prisoner intent on stalking should be denied the ability to inflict continued misery on a victim from within custody. While there is little hard evidence as yet of the scope of this problem the use of latest technology will help minimize any risk to victims. A program of installation of the new technology across the prison system is scheduled to begin later this year."[96]

Piloted at Full Sutton Prison near York, it keenly monitors prisoner telephone use, while permitting legitimate contact with the outside world. This new system provides prisoners with pre-approved numbers and a personal identification number. It is planned to be installed by mid-1999, starting with the highest security prisons.

In some states, the victim or victims family will be notified if the stalker is released from jail or prison, for example this is the case in California. "A victim, family member or witness may request that the California Department of Correction, county sheriff or the director of the local department of corrections notify them by phone or mail 15 days before a convicted stalker is released from jail or prison. The victim, family member or witness must keep these departments notified of their most current mailing address and telephone number. The information relating to persons who receive notice must be kept confidential and not released to the convicted stalker. (California Penal Code 646.92) The court may order a person convicted of felony stalking to register with local law enforcement officials within 14 days of moving to a city and/or county. (California Penal Code 646.9).[97]

In Michigan the juvenile's family was informed they would be notified if the stalker was released. As it turned out, they were not informed. They only learned of his release when the stalker renewed his pursuits.

Even though the stalker is incarcerated, the stress for the victim may not end. Steven Spielburg was concerned that even though his stalker would be locked up for a while, when he got out might still go after him. "But even knowing that Norman will be locked away for a good long time might not be enough for the famed filmmaker. "I'm very distraught over the possibility that this man could come out of jail and go right back on the warpath again," Spielburg said last October. "It's become an emotional obsession with me." [98]

The threat of police apprehension and ultimately imprisonment may not deter a stalker determined to punish a victim for real or imagined offenses. Nor would it deter a stalker who is willing to die to achieve his objective.

CHAPTER 8
LOOKING FORWARD- WHAT NEEDS TO BE DONE

Law enforcement officials work very hard to keep us safe. However, they are reactive by nature, since they are called to the place of a crime, after its commission. Determining the occurrence of a crime and apprehending its culprits, are the provinces of law, not the future prediction of crime. The law is not a fortune teller; it can react only empirically, concerning conflict.

As time goes on and a stalking situation becomes more volatile and threatening, both the victim and their family must take steps, if they are ever to be secure. Victims and family members always have to be on their guard and ready to protect themselves. Victims often feel a great deal of anger in these situations. They are angry with themselves and with the stalker. The uselessness of guilt and blame have no place in rendering a happy life for these individuals. Their normal life is interrupted and blasted by a criminal, who forces himself onto them, not vice-versa. They just want to lead normal happy lives with their families, but instead they live in fear. Fear is the goal of the stalker, who alone is guilty and deserving punishment.

So what needs to be done? Victims need to be familiar with possible stalking situations and their remedies. First, victims must ignore feelings of guilt; second, they must aid the police in every way possible; third, they must work with the prosecutor until the stalker is reproved to the limit of the law. Only if stalking is treated seriously by both victim and law enforcement, will it end or be curtailed; any other attitude jeopardizes society and mocks propriety. Even though

132

many cases are not true stalking cases, each case needs to be taken seriously and evaluated for its authenticity.

Since many of us don't really think anything bad will happen, we tend to be more trusting of individuals than we should be. We are hearing more and more about trusting our instincts. This advice should be taken to heart. If someone or a situation makes a victim feel uncomfortable they should get as far away from it as they can. Unfortunately, it is not always that simple. In Joan's case, her stalker was on the quiet side. Her instincts were telling her something wasn't quite right but she attributed this to his being shy, and therefore not seeing the problem. To help ourselves from being stalked we need to be more cautious about who we want to have relationships with. Don't take someone's behavior or what they say at face value. This isn't advice to make people feel paranoid or to keep them from having relationships. It's to help individuals from becoming stalking victims.

I believe as more cases come out, and the more educated we become, stalking will be taken seriously. By educating ourselves, police, prosecutors and judges will we see this happen. Don't be discouraged. Stalking is a horrible crime, but there are many that survive such situations. "The homicide rate among victims of stalking is less than 2%"[99]

We've taken a positive step by enacting antistalking laws. Stalking, ironically, may shatter lives, without breaking laws!
In the past, law enforcement had to wait until a physical attack occurred before being able to take action. Now the antistalking statutes can be used to decide if an arrest should be made. With the enactment of the laws, law enforcement officials can use the laws to

intervene before violence or death occurs.

"As police and prosecutors learn more about the availability and applicability of antistalking laws, the impact of the legislation is likely to increase" [100]

There are those who say that the overall effectiveness of stalking laws remain with the courts. Judges have many concerns: keeping the public safe, incarcerating the stalker, and nullifying bogus charges based on revenge. The public perception and overcrowded prisons are also in the mix. However, true victims warrant help, and the legal professions are mandated to give it! For the laws to be effective, police, judges and the populace must see the crime as serious, not frivolous. Some may die. "Their legal responsibility must be guided primarily by the nature of the act and the seriousness of the threat and they must be willing to properly sentence and restrain offenders who stalk." [101]

There have been complaints about the sentencing decisions of judges in stalking cases, since many of the decrees are either too lenient or simply dismissive. It has been said that judges do not truly understand the impact of a stalking situation. However, this is not always the case. In Santa Ana California a 40 year old woman stalked a man, five years younger than her, who had spurned her. (Again, stalkers are both genders!) The stalker told him that she might burn down his house and take his young son. She threatened to kill him. She falsely reported the victim as a child molester. She also had his electricity shut off and changed his telephone number. The stalker maintained her innocence throughout the trial. She even apologized to the victim at the hearing. She said she didn't know what possessed her to do the things she did and that she didn't mean to be malicious.

The stalker was sentenced to five years in prison. Three years of the term had to be served in a state prison. The rest of the term had to be served in the county jail.

Along with lenient sentences, another complaint is when a protective order is authorized. Civil courts do not have access to the criminal records of the accused. When the judge reviews the protective order application, he may not be aware of the accused's criminal history or outstanding arrest warrants. As a result, the correct action against an offender is not given. The victim has to start all over again.

Law enforcement officers need to encourage victims to make police reports. They should recommend that victims document any contact whatsoever with the stalker. This documentation will assist police, judges, prosecutors and psychiatrists to achieve maximum results in arresting, convicting or committing the stalker.

The new antistalking legislation provides the tools for law enforcement to protect victims from inappropriate contact. Unfortunately laws alone don't always protect victims. Criminals, by definition, are *lawbreakers*; therefore, the number of laws on the books is inconsequential. It is their constant and consistent enforcement, which will frustrate and waylay the criminal! Nevertheless, again victims—both actual and potential—must do all they can in helping themselves first, before the law enters to end the problem. By educating ourselves on what stalking is and what can be done about it can only benefit all parities involved.

It is clear that many stalking victims are not receiving the help they desperately need and are searching for. Law enforcement can only do so much. Victims need to take control of their own lives as much as they can. They may not be able to control the actions of the stalker but can take action to control their own lives. There are certain safety precautions--some drastic, others not—that the victim may choose as best for them. The strategy of the victim is a very individualized program. Apart from legal maneuvers, the plot to disengage a stalker must be quite personal. Victims have to decide what action is best for them.

Also, since stalking laws are new and there are different responses to them, victims should use whatever laws work best for their specific circumstances. Make our laws work for you. Use trespass laws instead of PPO's to prosecute, if that is what it takes to get a serious response from the authorities.

Not everyone has to completely change his or her identity. But one thing for sure is that once a person is stalked, their lives will never be completely the same again. Often the victim feels unnecessary and uncontrollable blame and guilt about her plight, and that of the family, while fearing the loss for general safety, welfare, and authority over their lives. Nonetheless, the good news is that there is hope for the future. Astute education and pointed law enforcement will combine against the criminal while combining for the victim. The more serious society inspects stalking, the quicker will be the stalkers incarceration. For the stalker, the future looks bleak indeed!

Victims can combat this problem by dealing with it in an intelligent manner, which consists of personal discipline, legal machinery, and tenacious prosecutions. This is shown by defining stalking, knowing the law, and insistence upon legal retribution. Through such a process, the victim and the law may work in a tandem. There is no room for shoddy or haphazard maneuvering in this procedure.

Progress is being made to help victims. The National Criminal Justice Association, for instance, has suggested that state legislatures should make it difficult for stalkers to locate their victims. This could be done by tightening confidentiality requirements on voter registration and motor vehicle information. Federal legislators have discussed limiting the amount of information available from other agencies, as well.

There are prevention strategies in the works. "Appending bill in Florida would hike the penalty for stalkers who use public records to trace their victims". [102] Regarding individual states, Massachusetts sets an example by having computerized all records of restraining orders and violations. This enables police officers or judges to cross-reference them to pinpoint habitual offenders.

The idea of having victims and stalkers wear electronic monitoring devices, similar to those used in house arrest cases, is being used in some states. Should a stalker come within a certain range of the victim, an alarm would automatically sound. Currently, Michigan is using electronic monitoring devices on domestic violence and stalking offenders. The technique has been effective in protecting victims.

Another positive aspect is that due to the 1994 Crime Bill by the U.S. Congress, the tracking and compilation of stalking crime statistics are now mandated. This means that experts will be able to determine the universality of this crime for the first time. In doing so, further assistance may be available to stalking victims.

We are just starting to learn and understand the full horror of the crime of stalking. There are many factors to this crime that we don't know. "It is unknown how many stalkings result in murder, how many victims are able to elude their stalkers by relocating or changing their identities, how many stalkers eventually stop pursuing their target in the absence of legal interventions, and how many stalkers choose new targets." [102]

Also, it's been difficult to determine to what extent laws are being used, if they're being used with other statutes and exactly how effective they are. "Currently, there is little hard data, however, on how many stalkers and victims are former intimates, how many murdered women were stalked beforehand or how many stalking incidents overlap with domestic violence" [103]

However research is being conducted to further the protection of the victims, in addition to finding the means and punishment for the crime itself. Victims say it's not their fault. The fault lies with the stalker. Stalking is a problem of society. Stalkers need to be made accountable for their actions. Only an informed, brave network of allies and families have the strength to stop the stalker. The network has to be powerfully motivated in the goal of ending the "reign of terror", that the stalker has formed. While the laws are maturing, they have not yet reached their full potential.

In addition to notifying the authorities, if someone suspects that they are being stalked, they should immediately request assistance from their local victim specialists in developing a safety plan. Victim specialists can be contacted at local rape crisis or domestic violence programs along with the victim's assistance coordinator in the prosecutor's office. These should be listed in the front section of the phone book under Emergency Assistance Numbers.

Taking safety precautions, moving, relocating, and going into hiding is troublesome for the victim. The victim is the innocent party and the stalker is the problem. The victim's rights are violated, but the stalker goes free. It is unfair. Should the victim move or relocate? These are choices the victim has to make. They are not easy. All crime, by its heinous nature, is unfair. The victim must understand this, and use intelligence to stop the stalker. If the victim or the victim's loved ones are in danger, the decision must be thought out and started on immediately, based upon sound legal advice. The choice has to be with the victim; each situation is unique. Until our criminal justice professionals completely understand the ramifications of stalking and deals with stalkers effectively, we must take whatever steps necessary to keep ourselves safe. Understand that it can happen to anyone- and it does.

Based on the information that I have offered, the reader must decide on the appropriate course of action to take. Weigh all the choices and alternatives carefully. Through research, I know that stalkers make their victims' lives hell and may even kill their victims. I've also learned that people who are stalked can survive and go on to lead fulfilling lives. KNOW THAT YOU ARE NOT ALONE AND THERE IS HELP FOR YOU. Never give up. Balance risk with safety.

Some of the cases mentioned began before stalking laws went into effect. Those individuals have survived and moved on. Now, we have stalking laws that can and has helped many people. The laws combined with our education on stalking, are catalysts in the war against stalkers, and lost battles are turning into winning victories for the victims!

I hope this book gave the reader some sense of how reprehensible the crime of stalking can be. It is a terrible, physical and psychological crime. But at the same time, I want to show the reader that stalking victims can persevere, and go on with successful lives. They still can take care of their families and themselves. I also want to suggest that stalkers eventually will pay a tremendous price for their deviations, and that the law is on the side of the victim. It is comforting to remember that the strength of the human spirit goes on. I've seen people go on despite life's shattering obstacles.

The victims in this book didn't do anything that the reader can't do.

They survived.

REFERENCES

1.   Stalking in America: Findings From the National Violence Against Women Survey. Patricia Tjaden and Nancy Thoennes, April 1998 169592.txt at www.ncjrs.org

2.   National Institute of Justice, Project To Develop a Model Anti-Stalking Code for States. National Criminal Justice Association. October 1993

3.   1994 CIS Annual Legislative Histories of US Public Laws, Violenct Crime Control and Law Enforcement Acct of 1994

4.   Threatening and Otherwise Inappropriate Letters to Hollywood Celebrities, Dietz, P.E., Matthews, D.B, Journal of Forensic Sciences, JFSCA, Vol. 36, No.1, Jan. 1991, pp.185-209

5.   Dietz, P.E., Matthews, D.B., "Threatening and Otherwise Inappropriate Letters to Members of the United States Congress". Journal of Forensic Sciences, JFSCA, Vol. 36, No. 5, Sept. 1991, pp.1445-1468

6.   Fein, Robert A., Vossekuil, Bryan, Holden, Gwen A. "Threat Assessment: An Approach To Prevent Targeted Violence" July 1995,

7.   Zona, Michael A., Sharma, Kaushal K., Lane, John. "A Comparative Study of Erotomanic and Obsessional Subjects in a Forensic Sample", Journal of Forensic Sciences, JFSCA, Vol. 38, No. 4, July 1993, pp. 894-903

8.   Toobin, Jeffrey. "Stalking In L.A." The New Yorker, February 24 & March 3, 1997

9.   Sherman, William. "Stalking: The Nightmare That Never Ends" Cosmpolitan, April 1994 v216 n4 p 198(4)

10.   National Victim Center, "Safety Strategies For Stalking Victims". **http://www.nvc.org/gdir/svsafety.htm**

11.   National Victim Center, "Questions and Answers".

http://www.nvc.org/ddir/info43.htm
12. Leong, G.B., "De Clerambault Syndrome (Erotomania) in the Criminal Justice System: Another Look at this Recurring Problem" Journal of Forensic Sciences, JFSCA, Vol.39, No ,2 (March 1994), p 378-385
12.   Jordan, Tatia. *The Efficacy of the California Stalking Law: Surveying Its Evolution, Extracting Insights from Domestic Violence Cases.* Copyright 1995 Hastings College of the Law. Jordan.html at www.uchastings.edu
13.   Gross, Linden. "Twisted love: a deadly obsession", Cosmopolitan, July 1992 v213, n1 p190(4)
14.   Ayoob, Massad. "I'm Being Stalked! Can you help me?", Shooting Industry, April 1994 v39 n4 p28(2)
15.   Serant, Claire. "Stalked; any women can be a victim of this heinous crime", Essence, Oct 1993 v24 n6 p72(9)
16.   Gill, Mark S. "The phone stalkers", Ladies Home Journal, Sept 1995 v112 n9 p82(5)
17.   House Legislative Analysis Section. Stalking. House Bill 5472 (Substitute H-4), Sponsor: Rep. Dianne Byrum; Huse Bill 6038 (Substitute H-1), Sponsor: Rep. Dianne Byrum; Senate Bill 719 (SubstituteH-4) Sponsor: Senator Robert Geake. First Analysis (9-16-92); Committee: Judiciary; Senate Committee (Sb719): Judiciary.
18.   Kaplan, Steve. "Questions and Answers on Michigan's New Anti-Stalking Legislation". Oakland Bar Association, February 1994
19.   National Victim Center, Infolink, Volume 1, No. 43, 1994
20.   Gross, Linden. To Have Or To Harm, Warner Books, 1994
21.   Mair, George. Star Stalkers, Pinnacle Books, 1995
22.   "Man Guilty of E-Mail 'Stalking'", Copyright 1996 by the Associated Press
23.   The National Victim Center, Interstate Stalking Punishment and Prevention Act of 1996. Introduced by Rep. Ed Royce, of

California, on Feb. 28, 1996. As of April 10, 1996, pending in the House Judiciary Committee.

24.　Quigley, Paxton. Not An Easy Target.　Fireside, Simon &Schuster, Inc. 1995

25.　S.O.S. Survivors Of Stalking, Ending The Silence That Kills, I d e n t i f y i n g　I f　Y o u ' r e　A　v i c t i m . **http://www.gate.net/~soshelp/two.htm**

27.Privacy Rights Clearinghouse, Fact Sheet #14: Are You Being Stalked?, Tips for Protection. 21 January 1997 Copyright 1994, 1995 1996 1997. Utility Consumers' Action Network

28.　Butchart, Alex, Motingoe, N., & Mabogoane, M., "RISK FACTORS FOR DOMESTIC VIOLENCE AGAINST WOME: SOME PRELIMINARY DATA", UNISA Health Psychology Unit and Centre for Peace Action

29.　El Gaddal, Y.Y., "De Clerambault's Syndrome (Erotomania) in Organic Delusional syndrome", British Journal of Psychiatry (1989), 154, 714-716

30.　Harmon, R.B., Rosner, R., and Owens, H., "Obsessional Harassment and Erotomania in a Criminal court Population", Journal of Foresic Sciences, JFSCA, Vol. 40, No. 2, March 1995, pp. 188-196

31.　"Women don't escape workplace violence, study says", USA TODAY, Health, by the Associated Press

32.　Gargan, J.P. "Stop stalkers before they strike", Security Management, Feb. q1994,v38, n2 p31 (3)

33.　Morales, Dan Attorney. LegalMatters, "Stalking Law" May 1997

34.　Stalking Laws, Transcripst September15, 1997 9a.m.-10a.m., Copyright 1997 by the Courtroom Television Network.

35.　Workplace Violence, Before, During, and After, Heskett, S.L., Copyright 1996 by Butterworth-Heinemann

36.　U.S. Department of Justice, Domestic violence and Stalking,

The Second annual Report to congress under the Violence Against women Act, violence Against Women Grants Office, July 1997

37.   Project To Develop a Model Anti-Stalking Code for States,, National Institute of Justice, October 1993

38.   Moret, Jim. "Technology brings stalkers one step closer to celebrities", CNN, 1997 Cable New

39.   Lefevre, Greg. "Guarding privacy tougher as Internet expands" CNN, 1996 Cable News Network Inc.

40.   Fields-Meyer, Thomas, Vicki Sheff-Cahan, "The Defenders", People, October 19, 1998, pp. 149-151

41.   Woman Sentenced to Five Years In Prison for Stalking Man. 16 May 1996. Copyright 1994-1997 San Diego Daily Transcript

42.   Violent Crime Control and Law Enforcement Act of 1994. 1994 CIS Annual Legislative Histories of U.S. Public Laws. September 13, 1994

43.   Blackwell, Jo Ann. "Stalking and Harassment on E-Mail and Internet". **http://www.cs.unca.edu/ blackwja/ethic.html**

44.   Anti-Stalking Bill Becomes Law. 1996 National Women's Health Resource Center.

45.   "What to do if you are being stalked?" British Columbia, Ministry of Women's Equality, Ministry of Attorney General

46.   Riley, Claudette. "Man convicted of stalking K-State student". Copyright 1995, Student Publications, Inc. 27 October 1995

RESOURCES

1.   Survivors of Stalking
      P.O. Box 20762
      Tampa, FL 33622
      Phone: (813) 889-0767

2.   National Organization for victim Assistance (NOVA)
      1757 park
      N.W. Washington, D.C. 20010
      Phone: (202) 232-6682
      Hotline: (800) 879-6682
      E-mail: **nova@access.digex.net**

3.   National Domestic Violence Hotline
      3616 Far West Blvd
      No. 101-297
      Austin, TX 78731
      24-hour hotline; (800) 799-SAFE
      TDD Phone: (800) 787-3224

4.   National Victim Center
      2111 Wilson Blvd
      Ste. 300
      Arlington, VA 22201
      Phone: (800) FYI-CALLor
      (703) 276-2880

5.   National Criminal Justice Association
      444 N. Capitol Street, NW, Ste. 618

Washington, DC 20001
Phone: (202) 624-1440
Fax: (202) 508-3859
e-mail: **ncja@sso.org**

6.   Gavin de Becker Incorporated
11684 Ventura Boulevard
Ste. 440
Studio City
California 91604
e-mail: **infoline@gdbinc.com**

7.   Stalking Victims Sanctuary
e-mail: **assistance@stalkingvictims.com**

Other Resources

1. **http://www.cyberangels.org/stalking/index.html**
2. http://www.cyberangels.org/chatsmarts.html#harass

[1] DeBecker, Gavin. The Gift of Fear. Little, Brown and Company, 1997 pp. 183-184

[2] National Institute of Justice, Tjaden, Patricia. "The Crime of Stalking: How Big Is The Problem?". November 1997. P 2 fs000186.txt at www.ncjrs.org

[3] National Institute of Justice, Domestic Violence, Stalking, and Antistalking Legislation, An Annual Report to Congress under the Violence Against Women Act, April 1996. p 4

[4] Funk and Wagnalls Standard Desk Dictionary, Volume I. Lippincott & Crowell, Publishers, Copyright 1980.

[5] Jane McAllister, Hearing Before The Committee On The Judiciary United States Senate, One Hundred Second Congress

[6] Jane McAllister, Hearing BeforeThe Committee On The Judiciary United States Senate, One Hundred Second Congress

[7] National Institute of Justice, Domestic Violence, Stalking, and Antistalking Legislation, p6

[8] Ibid

[9] Ibid

[10] Hathaway, Don Sheriff.Caddo Parrish Sheriff's Office. :Are You A Stalking Target?" http://www.caddosheriff.org/index-1.htm

[11] Funk & Wagnalls, Standard Desk Dictionary Volume2.Lippincott & Crowell, Publishers, Copyright 1980

[12] Bureau of Justice Statistics, Special Report, National Crime Victimiztion Survey, Warchol, Greg. "Workplace Violence, 1992-1996".

[13] Hearing Before The committee on The Judiciary, United States Senate, One Hundred Second Congress, Second Session. S.2922

[14] National Institute of Justice, Tjaden, Patricia. "The Crime of Stalking: How Big Is The Problem?". November 1997. P 3 fs000186.txt at www.ncjrs.org

[15] McClear, James A., Mike Martindale. "Protection orders easy to obtain, often overused". Detroit News, 23 July 1998

[16] Meloy, Reid J. The Psychology of Stalking. Academic Press, 1998, p 79

[17] Brown, Lou, Francois Dubau and Merritt McKeon. Stop Domestic Violence. St. Martin's Press. April 1997. P 28

[18] Dr. Gary Kaufmann, Chief Psychologist, Michigan State Police Behavioral Science Section, Interview 1996

[19] Ibid

[20] Meloy, Reid J. The Psychology of Stalking. Academic Press, 1998, p5

[21] Wallace, Harvey. Victimology. Allyn & Bacon. Copyright 1998. P 151

[22] National Institute of Justice, Tjaden, Patricia. "The Crime of Stalking: How Big Is The Problem?". November 1997. P 3 fs000186.txt at www.ncjrs.org

[23] Snow, Robert L. Stopping a Stalker. Plenum Trade, 1998, p 182

[24] Schaum Merlita, and Karen Parrish. Stalked. Pocket Books, 1995 p62

[25] Brown, Lou, Francois Dubau and Merritt McKeon. Stop Domestic Violence. St. Martin's Press. April 1997. P 28

[26] DeBecker, Gavin. The Gift of Fear. Little, Brown and Company, 1997. P 203

[27] Ibid p 198-199

[28] Ibid p 199-200

[29] National Institute of Justice, Tjaden, Patricia. "The Crime of Stalking: How Big Is The Problem?". November 1997. P 2 fs000186.txt at **www.ncjrs.org**

[30] Hearing Before the Committee On The Judiciary United States Senate, September 29, 1992

[31] Zona, M. A., Sharma, K.K., and Lane, J., "A Comparative Study of Erotomanic and Obsessional Subjects in a Forensic Sample," Journal of Forensic Sciences, JFSCA, Vol. 38, No. 4 July 1993, pp. 894-903

[32] Brenner, Marie. "Erotomania". Vanity Fair, September 1991

[33] Orion, Doreen. I Know You Really Love Me. Macmillan USA, 1997, p 19-20

[34] Bonnie Campbell, Director, Violence Against Women Office, U.S. Department of Justice. Letter to me, 1997

[35] Meloy, Reid J. The Psychology of Stalking. Academic Press, 1998 p58

[36] Ibid p 6

[37] Marino, Thomas W. "Looking over your shoulder". Counseling Today, October 1995

[38] Ibid

[39] Ibid

[40] Mr. Showbiz, Spielburg Stalker gets The Max, July 17, 1998

[41] Meloy, Reid J. The Psychology of Stalking. Academic Press, p57

[42] Dr. Gary Kaufmann, Chief Psychologist, Michigan State Police Behavioral Science Section, Interview 1996

[43] Ibid

[44] Ibid

[45] Meloy, Reid J. The Psychology of Stalking. Academic Press, 1998 p 4

[46] National Institute of Justice, Fein, Robert A. Bryan Vossekuil and Gwen A. Holden. "Threat Assessment: An Approach To Prevent Targeted Violence." July 1995

[47] DeBecker, Gavin. The Gift of Fear. Little, Brown and Company, 1997. Pp. 93-95

[48] National Institute of Justice, Tjaden, Patricia. "The Crime of Stalking: How Big Is The Problem?". November 1997. P 3-4 fs000186.txt at www.ncjrs.org

[49] Snow, Robert L. Stopping a Stalker. Plenum Trade, 1998, p 168

[50] Nancy Diehl, Assistant Prosecutor, Wayne County Michigan, Interview, 1996

[51] Bureau of Justice Assistance, Regional Seminar Series on Developing and Implementing Antistalking Codes, Monograph, June 1996 pp 14, 41

[52] National Institute of Justice, Domestic Violence, Stalking and Antistalking Legislation, p 6

[53] Melinda Beck with Debra Rosenberg in Boston, Farai Chideya in Chicago, Susan Miller in Houston, Donna Foote in Los Angeles, Howard Manly in Atlanta and Peter Katel in Tampa. "Murderous Obsession". Newsweek. 13 July 1992 p 61

[54] Ibid p 60

[55] Privacy Rights Clearinghouse, Fact Sheet # 14: Are You Being Stalked?, Tips for Protection. 21 January 1997 Copyright 1994, 1995 1996 1997. Utility Consumers' Action Network

[56] Michigan Law, Mighigan Penal Code MCLA 650.4 1 1 h

[57] National Institute of Justice, Domestic Violence, Stalking, and Antitstalking Legislation, An Annual Report to Congress under the Violence Against women Act, April 1996, p 7

[58] Bureau of Justice Assistance, Regional Seminar Series on Developing and Implementing Antistalking Codes, Monograph, June 1996 p 14

[59] Privacy Rights Clearinghouse, Fact Sheet # 14: Are You Being Stalked?, Tips for Protection. 21 January 1997 Copyright 1994, 1995 1996 1997. Utility Consumers' Action Network

[60] McClear, James A., Mike Martindale. "Protection orders easy to obtain, often overused". Detroit News, 23 July 1998
[61] Ibid
[62] Ibid
[63] Nancy Diehl, Assistant Prosecutor, Wayne County Michigan, Interview, 1996

[64] McClear, James A., Mike Martindale. "Protection orders easy to obtain, often overused". Detroit News, 23 July 1998

[65] Ibid
[66] DeBecker, Gavin. The Gift of Fear. Little, Brown and Company, 1997. P 188
[67]Geberth, Vernon J. "Stalking". Law and Order. October 1992, p 138
[68] DeBecker, Gavin. The Gift of Fear. Little, Brown and Company, 1997. P 142
[69] The National Victim Center, Stalking, Questions and Answers, "Are There Laws that Make Stalking A Crime?" **http://www.nvc.org/ddir/info43.htm** p5
[71] Ibid
[72] Ibid
[73] National Institute of Justice, Domestic Violence, Stalking, and Antitstalking Legislation, An Annual Report to Congress under the Violence Against women Act, April 1996, p 10 www.ncjrs.org

[74] National Victim Center The National Victim Center, Stalking, Questions and Answers, "Are There Laws that Make Stalking A Crime?" **http://www.nvc.org/ddir/info43.htm** p 5-6

[75] The National Victim Center. "Interstate Stalking Punishment and Prevention Act of 1996". Introduced by Rep. Ed Royce, of California, on Feb. 28, 1996. As of April 10, 1996, pending in the House Judiciary Committee.

[76] Top Issue. Safety and Security, At Home and Abroad. 23 September 1996

[77] National Victim Center The National Victim Center, Stalking, Questions and Answers, "Are There Laws that Make Stalking A Crime?" **http://www.nvc.org/ddir/info43.htm** p6

[78] National Victim Center The National Victim Center, Stalking, Questions and Answers, "Are There Laws that Make Stalking A Crime?" **http://www.nvc.org/ddir/info43.htm** p 7

[79] Snow, Robert L. Stopping a Stalker. Plenum Trade, 1998 p 199

[80] Snow, Robert L. Stopping a Stalker. Plenum Trade, 1998 p 198

[81] The Salt Lake Tribune. "Police Lending Phones to Stalking Victims. 19 February 1997. Copyright 1997, The Salt Lake Tribune

[82] Snow, Robert L. Stopping a Stalker. Plenum Trade, 1998 p 205

[83] Snow, Robert L. Stopping a Stalker. Plenum Trade, 1998 p 195

[84] Grant Jerding, USA Today, June 17,1998

[85] Scott, Michael. How To Lose Anyone Anywhere. Stealth Publishing, 1996. P 12-13

[86] The Detroit News. "E-mail stalker sentencing likely will influence future cases". 23 March 1996, Copyright 1996, The Detroit News

[87] Whitelaw, Kevin. "Fear and dread in cyberspace". U.S. News & World Report, 4 November 1996

[88] Blackwell, Jo Ann. "Stalking and harassment on E-Mail and Internet". http://www.cs.unca.edu/`blackwja/ethic.html
[89] Grossman, Mark. "Do Anti-Stalking Laws Apply in Cyberspace?" Copyright 1997 PC World Communications. February 1997
[90] Blackwell, Jo Ann. "Stalking and harassment on E-Mail and Internet". http://www.cs.unca.edu/`blackwja/ethic.html

[91] Hatcher, Colin Gabriel. "Cyberstalking Profiles". Copyright Colin Gabriel Hatcher
[92] DeBecker, Gavin. The Gift of Fear. Little, Brown and Company, 1997. P 199
[93] Snow, Robert L. Stopping a Stalker. Plenum Trade, 1998 p 188
[94] DeBecker, Gavin. The Gift of Fear. Little, Brown and Company, 1997. P 204
[95] [53] Melinda Beck with Debra Rosenberg in Boston, Farai Chideya in Chicago, Susan Miller in Houston, Donna Foote in Los Angeles, Howard Manly in Atlanta and Peter Katel in Tampa. "Murderous Obsession". Newsweek. 13 July 1992 p 61
[96] Penal Lexicon Home Page. "Joyce Quin, Announces Initiative To Counter Stalking From Within Prisons". 8 August 1997
[97] Privacy Rights Clearinghouse, Fact Sheet # 14: Are You Being Stalked?, Tips for Protection. 21 January 1997 Copyright 1994, 1995 1996 1997. Utility Consumers' Action Network p2
[98] Mr. Showbiz, Spielburg Stalker gets The Max, July 17, 1998

[99] Meloy, Reid J. The Psychology of Stalking. Academic Press, 1998 p 5
[100] National Institute of Justice, Domestic Violence, Stalking, and Antitstalking Legislation, An Annual Report to Congress under the Violence Against women Act, April 1996, p 8

101 67Geberth, Vernon J. "Stalking". <u>Law and Order</u>. October 1992, p 138-143

102 Carmody, Cristina. "Deadly Mistakes". <u>ABA Journal</u>. September 1994 p 71

103 National Institute of Justice, <u>Domestic Violence, Stalking, and Antitstalking Legislation</u>, An Annual Report to Congress under the Violence Against Women Act, April 1996 p 9 www.ncjrs.org

104 National Institute of Justice, <u>Domestic Violence, Stalking, and Antitstalking Legislation</u>, An Annual Report to Congress under the Violence Against Women Act, April 1996 p 3